ON BECOMING
HUMAN

ROSS SNYDER

On Becoming
Human

ABINGDON
NASHVILLE

ON BECOMING HUMAN

ISBN 0-687-28840-1

Library of Congress Catalog Card Number: 67-22162

MANUFACTURED BY THE PARTHENON PRESS AT
NASHVILLE, TENNESSEE, UNITED STATES OF AMERICA

TO
THE DESTINY GENERATIONS
WITH WHICH I PRESENTLY SHARE THIS
WORLD

CONTENTS

SECTION III

BRINGING OFF LIFE WORLDS

APPENDIX

A VOCABULARY WITH WHICH TO THINK AND TALK ABOUT HUMAN EXISTENCE

THIS BOOK AS A WAY OF THINKING
ABOUT BEING HUMAN

This is a book about becoming human. Something we are always about, but never finish. Something we always imperfectly realize. We continue to go off on detours, even demonic campaigns. But always there is a thrust toward it from within the pulsing of humane culture and from within us. We are fundamentally conceived to find life rather than death; fullness rather than emptiness.

A book can set out what the enterprise of establishing yourself as a human being is, what some of the basics and live options are, and how to work on them. That is as far as a book can go. Hopefully, this one is so written that it enables you to freshen and form your own life. That as you read you can call up the experiences you have had, and do the thinking that will enable you to become uniquely yourself in the nows and heres in which you situate your life. That you read not as a spectator, but as a participant in your one life on earth, reworking your possibilities as you read. "What is it to be human? My one life on earth— what making of it can I bring off?"

Like all other human beings, you live out of *expectations*. You have energy only insofar as you expect that something *will* come off. Only insofar as the future you see for yourself is tinged with hope and filled with some promise. No one can survive outside a mood of expectancy.

An expectation has two dimensions—something is desirable, *and* you also believe it will come off. You believe that it is possible, not just a fanciful daydream or idealistic something which will never come by sea or land.

So an expectancy is a realistic goal which lets loose energy inside you. With expectancy you believe that—the world being what it is—the enterprise of your life will come off. At least it has a fighting chance. And you don't have the awful feeling that *everything* depends on you. You can count on powers other than just yourself.

So it is a good thing, once in a while, to center down on "What do I *expect* of life? What does life expect of me?" That too is what this book is about.

We all operate with many little, short-term life goals. But it is the large hunch—"life is in this direction, rather than in these other directions"—that we need. We need to find big enough goals that they never are finished; goals big enough that whatever happens, we can land on our feet in any situation.

So, in the following chapters we are trying for a life that you won't have to feel uncertain and apologetic about. A life that has a rightness to it because it is the way people become persons. The chapters are not just about what you might be, or "it would be nice if I were this." They are a statement of what you are *if* you are a person. They attempt to describe the way man constitutes himself.

You could be resolute about such existence. For you

would be *actualizing* life. You would be an agent—rather than a patient—of civilization.

If I were asked to give a name to the viewpoint presented in this book, I would christen it "a religious existential-phenomenological-developmental way of being-in-the-world." If this begins to come through to you by the time you have wrestled your way through the book, we will both have done well.

DIGGING INTO A CHAPTER

If a chapter particularly interests you, here is a way of getting what it offers in some depth—

1. A situation I've been in that the chapter is dealing with.

   How is it with me in regard to the most interesting point of the chapter?

2. The one sentence that makes the main point of the chapter. How would I say it in the words I use to think, feel, decide with?

   The sequence of ideas which is the line of thought.

3. Can I use the viewpoint presented, someplace it would make a difference?

It may be most profitable to kick the chapter around with some other person that you enjoy talking with. Whose judgment you respect and causes you to think furiously.

A VOCABULARY OF WORDS FOR THINKING "HUMAN EXISTENCE"

One other understanding between you and the book may be helpful.

Some of the important words in it may be new to you —or used with fresh meanings.

This is an important aspect of this book. Some words we commonly use are ordinary, mediocre. And are worn so smooth that they pass right through our minds and mouths without ever stirring thought. Other great words have become trivialized. Some we have never stopped to think what they mean—for example, little but significant words like "with" and "for." Some few words are packed full of meaning. They explode when you really get them. They provide working capital for the rest of your life. Because they have this depth, you don't get inside them easily. But life is there, waiting for you.

Freshening up your vocabulary is one way of becoming more of a person. New words enable us to be sensitive to whole new areas of life that we previously never even knew existed. And if we are going to be *contemporary,* we need to possess *now* the words that the present deepest thinking about life is being done with. Get in on the excitement as it is happening!

None of us can be alive today with an impoverished mind.

You learn a fresh word by watching when people use it, and then connecting it with some experience of yours, until it lights up and you see there greater depth yet to explore. This also only you can do. You need to get it defined so that it has some *definite* meaning. So you know what is being said, what is not being said, and how it differs from the sloppy misconceptions many people have of the concept. To help this happen for you—and as a help in my own thinking clearly—I have put together a sort of dictionary of the words that carry the major meanings of "being human." You will find it at the end of the book for handy reference, both while you read and afterward.

For exploring, thinking, organizing one's self as a becoming-human, continues all through life. There is always more to understand, and to be. Events and inventions we never dreamed of come at us and set problems we have never solved. We keep working at it—and therefore stay alive.

Section I

YOU AS LIFE WORLD
THE TWO POLES

1

BRING OFF A LIFE WORLD

You were meant to be. It is right for you to be fully alive.

NO ONE ELSE CAN DO IT FOR YOU

You were not born for the purpose of obeying someone else, or being a branded member in a herd. You were born to become a unique, particular expression of human being. And you are the only one who can make something of your one life on earth.

You had nothing to say about where and when you were born, or of what parents. And all your life, world events and situations not of your own making will set conditions in which you must make your way. But you remain in charge of your decisions and what you intend to mean in those events.

To bring off a life is neither simple or easy. Depth and direction are crucial.

Depth comes from intense experiencing and the richness of interpretation you make of it. From moments of agony and of fulfillment. From aloneness and from being united with others.

Direction comes from what's going on in the world and

the live options you vision, into which you throw your energies with exuberance and long-term fidelity.

So long as you are human, you live with goals and imaged futures toward which you stretch yourself. Your imagination—your power to sense potential and imagine possibility—is one secret of your growing.

LIFE SPACE AND LIFE WORLD

As a human being, you are surrounded by—you are in—*life* space. All the persons and things of the universe are invitations to relationship and to action. They offer futures to you—if only you can see them. In this particular moment of mankind, the offerings are staggering in range and possibility.

Out of all this you have to choose a few persons, a few enterprises that you can develop in depth. For you are limited. You can't do everything; you can't be everything. You have to become *some* thing, something *in particular*. You hope, significantly so.

So all your life you probe this life space. You try to find openings in it where there is room for you to actualize your life. You select out some persons and enterprises to be part of. You test out ways of relating to them. You continually organize a *life* world.

Some persons and enterprises you are for—they are life for you. Others are death and nothingness for you. They numb you, diffuse you, disintegrate you, poison your powers of self-propulsion, dull your sensitivities, shut you off from lively people, mislead you down a path which is only a dead end. They hold you to being a static, uncaring person.

Gradually you build up a *life* world which, for you, is

your destiny in this world. It is the arena where you play out the struggle of life versus death for you. The rest of your life space becomes background. This life world becomes the foreground and pioneer settlement of your life.

A THRUST THAT INCLUDES ALL OTHER GOALS

Organizing a life world and taking it someplace is what life is about. It is the goal that includes all other goals.

For no person exists in and of himself. You exist physically only as you are immersed in an ocean of life-giving air. You exist as man only because you have participated from the moment of birth in a world of human beings and culture. You are a self-in-a-world, not just a self. "To be" is not you *and* the world. Your membership in the world is symbolized by a hyphen rather than by "and."

"To be" means to co-create a *life world*.

Not that you own it, or that it is all your making. But you have poured enough of your life into it that your values have soaked into it; your footprints, telling that a human has been here, can be seen; your song can be heard in its valleys and mountaintops. For you it is saturated with memories and mystery.

It has become your habitat. The territory you *in*-habit—which you would defend with your life against destroyers. The place where the story of your life is inserted into some larger history.

THE HYPOTHESIS

"To actualize" life is to bring off a life world. This is what you are doing, whether you know it or not.

2

BE ALIVENESS

LIFE IS A POLARITY

Within your life world, you are meant to be a center of aliveness. An originating center that uniquely sees and feels the world, manufactures meanings, invents possibilities. You are a center of decision and fidelity over a period of time. An *agent* of life, not just a resentment against life or a taking it on the chin from life.

While you do not exist *apart from* your life world, you are a *self*-in-world.

All life consists of two poles—you as centered self and the rest of your life world (what we usually call "the world").

Both poles need to be potent if much is to happen.

DEVELOP AND FEED YOUR ALIVENESS

So one of the goals of life is to nurture yourself as a center of aliveness, origination, meaning. Each of us is to act responsibly toward his own becoming. And not act as if he expected to have it done for him and *to* him. As if it were somebody else's responsibility to make him what he ought to be. Or that it can be *done* that way.

This responsibility for one's own becoming, this nurturing of one's self into being deeply, warmly, richly a person is not the same as selfishness. Although it could be deflected into selfishness.

Properly it is taking seriously the parable of the talents. You are lacking respect for yourself, your fellow man, and God when you wrap your talent (your potential for becoming effectively personal) up in a lily-white napkin and bury it so that it never develops or becomes manifest. You are unfaithful when your energies are absorbed in justifying yourself as you are, in defending and protecting yourself from risk. Frustrating your becoming, you sicken and find yourself in inner darkness.

BECOMING AND DEVELOPING IS WHAT YOU ARE AND MUST BE

Implanted in the stuff of all life is one urge—*the drive of potential to become actual,* i.e., to take shape and realize its potential. This fundamental drive you cannot violate with impunity. But you can count on it. As a human being, you are to some degree in charge of it.

A built-in goal of life then is that you actualize your potential in the heres and nows given you. You have been given the possibility of becoming fully personal. Do you importantly intend to do something about it?

One of man's grave sins is the sin of not being, of never having been born. Of being "a faceless one" with no boundaries, no distinctive contours, no mouth that speaks nor eyes that invite. Equally damnable is the life that refuses to be reborn. That regards itself as finished.

The medieval ages thought of everything—the world of nature and the world of human society—as essentially

21

finished. All that was left to each generation was to endure more of the same and faithfully live out its lot in life, using religion as *a way out* of what was. In all areas of thought today, there is a view of life as becoming and developing new ideas instead of this static and finished world view. People are now beginning to live within this new view, even in their personal lives. You are to become more than you now are. By nature you are not merely a center, but a *becoming* center. It is all too easy to be part of the fallen ones—those who see themselves as finished, who have a vicious need to keep everybody down to their level and put the blame for themselves upon others. They see themselves as a *product* —of their family, their school, their time in civilization —rather than as energy on its way to becoming more than it now is. Ultimately they become fat around the middle and in the head. They serve as a front for other people's desires, but they themselves are vegetables.

Prophetic religion has been concerned through the ages about this condition of man. Prophets have shouted to their fellow men to run from it. They have offered transformation and a promise of new life. For the truth about the God the prophets know is: "Behold, I will do a new thing; now it shall spring forth" (Isa. 43:19).

When it has been true to the New Testament, Christianity has always testified to the inbreaking kingdom of God—which is here on earth in power, but not yet in its fullness.

Becoming is the very nature of aliveness. Restlessness is at the core of all human history. As persons, we are alive only in the moment of some fresh birthing of ourselves. We are alive in some growing edge of our life; we rot away when no movement is happening within and we are no longer diving deep into life.

Becoming is not identical with just any change or any "This is new." To be blown hither and yon by the winds of current fashion is not *becoming*. Becoming suggests a leap up into a new level of consciousness. It suggests a directedness toward something, rather than successively zooming off in all directions. It points to cumulative development, not just an adding on of a new detail or experience. The person of religious faith has some guidance for his becoming. For today he holds a doctrine of continuing creation, and his question is, "What new possibility is God offering in this immediate situation, in this moment of history-making?" The answer his life makes to this question determines his becoming.

Becoming also says that the new takes on *significant form*. Becoming is not the same as swinging wild energies on the loose, irresponsibility running rampant on a pleasure binge, a motorcycle devouring space. When it is *becoming*, the fresh vitality takes *pattern*. It takes on *style*. By "style" now meaning not fashion, but a mobilization of energy that simply and effectively does what is relevant in the situation. In this sense, Christian style is ultimate morality and the maturity of becoming.

We have been talking about you as a center of aliveness. Or more accurately, a center of *becoming aliveness*. We have been talking about you as responsible for feeding, nurturing, developing this aliveness.

Where are you alive, rather than a blob of nothingness? What constitutes *aliveness*?

Section II

YOU AS A CENTER
OF ALIVENESS

3

CARING AND FEELING DEEPLY

What creates you as aliveness?

The primary answer is—"to be caring." Sensitively engaged in what's happening. Not *cautious* about life, but interested in *nurturing* life.

Caring is being intensely aware that life is here and now happening to you and to the things you are for. And you have an attitude toward those happenings. Caring means that you cherish some things, and that you are *for* the things you cherish. Not in a passive, sentimental way, but with considerable impact. Potential is in motion, and you give it the green light to a throughway.

Caring is your energies mobilized, interfused with deep feeling, engaged with the world—and it makes a difference to you how it comes out.

ALIVENESS IS WEALTH OF FEELING AND DEEPLY CARING

There's no virtue in being a clod. In going through life insensitive and with a poverty of experiencing. We need more feeling, more cultivation of sensitive awareness and valuing. It does not do to ignore this beginning aspect of our aliveness.

Therefore you should not be ashamed of having intense

feeling—but rather of its lack. And of your failure to interfuse the feelings you have with humane culture.

The ghastly grotesques of the twentieth century are the keepers of the gas chambers and concentration camps who trained themselves not to feel what was happening to other persons. Who tried to live insolently, arrogantly. And as machines efficient for the purposes set by The Party.

Love—in the deep sense we are now talking about—is the irreducible element which makes you a *human* being. It is an important measure of any person's greatness.

To feel, to have an attitude toward what is happening, is your first and last freedom as *man*.

As Viktor Frankl observed in concentration camp, when a person loses touch with how *he* actually feels about events and substitutes what other people tell him to feel, when his capacity to feel is eroded, when he loses his sense of being needed by some loved one, he quickly dies. For he has disintegrated *as a person*.

FEELING-CARING IS DIFFERENT FROM IMPULSE LIVING OR MERE EMOTION

Obviously "wealth of feeling and deeply caring" is something quite different from mere emotion or the impulse of the moment. Much human wreckage has happened because people did not know of the distinction. And thought they were living by feeling when they were expressing merely fragments and surfaces of life. Much "howl poetry," many "realistic" novels and movies, "new morality" ingroups mistake what feeling is.

Feeling is more than a sudden burst of emotion. It is not the same as jittery excitement. It is not a biological impulse harassing us.

It is a report *by the all of a person* on what kind of engagement he is having with the world.

And so feeling is *weather,* rather than one sprinkle of rain. More like a whole chord on guitar or piano than like a single note. More like a musical theme developing nuances of expression than eruptive pings, each starkly itself only. More like the heave of the tide or the ocean swell from the fury of an intercontinental storm than a ripple caused by a gust of wind.

Further, emotion and momentary surge of impulse tell us about *ourselves* more than about the total situation. They have little content of what is *out there.* Emotion and impulse specialize in the subjective (what *we* want) almost exclusively. They are not dependable reports of what we are participating in.

In contrast, feeling is report of *self-in-world.* Of *life world,* not just our inner condition and reaction. Feeling's organizer is the encounter, the engagement. The reality of the "out there" world is received and evaluated.

This means that feeling is always a result of a "dialogue" between tentative feeling *and understanding.* They both occur at once and determine each other. This makes feeling more accurate and relevant than emotion or impulse.

Feeling—contrary to some television shows, movies, paperbacks—is not just given by the biological body, although body is involved. "Body" has much more content.

Each of us is a bodied *self*. Or, if you prefer, a body interfused with self-awareness and culture.

Therefore, feeling is more than emotional disturbances set up by glandular secretions. Your self-concept or identity is also stirred up. Finally it has to be satisfied. Finally it throws the feeling switch.

Feeling—as contrasted with emotion—has these components of understanding and evaluation. Feeling is from *yourself as a whole person*. It includes what is often called the unconscious, but perhaps more properly termed the preconscious.

So most of us have learned to take the impulse, the surge of emotion (anger, defeat, sexuality, etc.), and let it work into what is more surely *feeling*. In feeling, we can have some confidence.

But even then, just because something "felt right" (so we thought) when we did it is no guarantee that it was the right thing to do. For always our understanding of the realities in the situation is involved. No feeling is "immaculately conceived." It is always influenced by our sensitivity to persons, by personal values, by pressures of some community we very much want to belong to. And in any given situation and movement all these may be badly mistaken. Even sick.

The life of feeling is *not* acting out whatever the impulse of the moment is. It is not life on a pleasure binge. It is not a life whose ruling principle is to avoid pain and struggle and conflict and striving over a period of time.

A nation can survive only if its people can endure through disasters and not give up because of pain. Civilization is possible only because some people are capable of the long pull. Society and person disintegrate when the prevailing feeling tone of their existence is, "It's easier to give up, quit trying. It's better to be a patient than an agent of my society." There is some hope for a nation only when the prevailing feeling tone is one of determination to match its powers against whatever the problem and play the part of men, demanding of the future that it hunger and thirst for justice.

NOTHING GOES ON IN US WITHOUT FEELING

Feeling is the ocean within us from which comes the meanings of our life. Without feeling, there would be no meaning. Feeling is before all thinking—a pulse of life deeper than we can ever consciously control or symbolize. It encompasses and interfuses all.

Feeling connects many different experiences over a period of time into a story of our life that is meaningful to us, puts what is now happening into its appropriate place. It brings together memories of past experiences, stirrings of our imagination toward futures, image of the people we are dealing with, ideas about the world and how it functions. And coheres all these into one womb out of which decision and action is born. Thus feeling both mobilizes us and births us.

It enables us to experience ourselves as a *self*. To know "I am." To sense our quality and significance.

Feeling is also our way of tuning into life around us. A mode of entering into the world. And an anchorage harbor from which we sail into and out of "the world out there."

So crucial is feeling, we should be much better friends of it than we are. Invite more feeling and enable it to become full and mature. To grow up into convictions.

Its central importance may come clearer by looking at two contrasting modes of feeling.

We can tune into life in a prevailing mood of celebration or tune out of life by a prevailing mood of resentment.

RESENTMENT IS ONE WAY OF TUNING IN TO LIFE

Resentment is a very complex feeling. It begins with a sense that one's dignity as a human being is being violated, one's right to be fully personal is denied. One feels treated as a thing—manipulated, used, treated as a satellite to some other person's whims, a mere appendage to his mind and plans.

We might escape our enslavement to resentment if we could voice this feeling of the situation and "have it out" with the person causing it. Resentment is compounded when we are afraid to do this, largely because we fear we would only be hurt further if we did. Or because we have been taught that we should never be angry; that it's wrong to feel as we do. Anyway, the person now hurting us (we feel) couldn't care less, is impervious to anything we say, will not listen. And we're not big enough to get through to him, force him to take account of us.

We begin to despise ourselves for not standing up for our rights, for being such weak, ineffectual persons unable to handle the situation. So we are now no longer "in cahoots" with ourselves; we are not tuned in. Resentment burns in an ever-revolving circle.

Finally we hate, withdraw from, try to destroy the society in which such things occur. And we hate, withdraw from, try to destroy ourselves.

Thus resentment is probably the major feeling disaster in a person's life. If it becomes a prevailing mood, it destroys all possibility of life world. A certain amount of it is almost an inevitable part of life, so we need to know how to work it through and again and again escape from its crippling bondage.

CELEBRATION IS TUNING IN

Radically different in quality and outcome is a prevailing (but not necessarily constant) mood of celebration. Celebration is appreciating the possibilities hidden in the folds of life, even while being aware of all the evil and frustration that is there. It is believing that creation has good in it, and this good we invoke. Celebration is delight in the elemental simplicities—the deed well done, the thought well spoken, the beauty freshly seen, the relation of intimacy, the imagination inventing new dreams, the conversation striking fire, the body exhilarated.

Celebration feeling is a *tuning in,* an entering into the life of the world in such a way as to sense the Holy. Its essence is stated in the famous phrase from the Catechism—

What is the chief end of man?
Man's chief end is to glorify God and to enjoy him forever.

Caring and deeply feeling is not necessarily a matter of going around feeling that life is an awful problem.

33

4

CHOOSING, DECIDING, TROTH

You are alive in moments of choosing and deciding.

Yes, it is often agony to decide. For we never know all that we need to know. About personally important matters we have to guess consequences rather than have proof. (Shall I marry the fellow or not? Is this really love?) We often have to give up some good for the sake of a better good. Sometimes this agony is so overwhelming that a person refuses to choose, opts out, declares a moratorium on choosing, lets whatever happens, happen.

But we are highly aware of ourselves in choosing, sometimes intensely alive. Surely more alive than in just sitting around rotting.

MUCH IS HAPPENING IN DECISION

To choose is to become aware of your values. Not to be aware of your values is to be not quite human. Not yet a *personal* aliveness.

Perhaps you are *significantly* alive *only* in moments of choice and decision. The rest of the time you are merely vegetating or biologically functioning.

For to choose and decide is to experience your self. To be present when you are creating yourself. And therefore to know "I am."

To choose and decide is to experience yourself as

person no longer hidden; but now in the open.
person searching for possibility and some way out.
person wrestling with fate.
person taking an attitude, intending something.
person living toward future.
person trying to define who and what he is.

These are all happening in a moment of decision.

Where else, then, other than in moments of important choice and decision would you find more of yourself seething like a volcano? More of yourself awakened? More fullness of lived moment?

These experiencings of yourself are existence situations. Moments when you are human. When *you* are. And you know it.

The pain and agony we all feel when we are unable to make up our minds is eloquent testimony on this point.

Indecision because we can't choose is awful. We feel that we are losing hold of ourselves. We can't collect the scattered bits of ourselves into focus; instead we are about to disintegrate and disappear. We are in process of ceasing to be. A loss of selfhood and an awful diffusing into nothingness takes over. Such is the horror of being unable to decide.

In choice and decision you are alive, even if you make wrong choices. However, it is true that wrong choices can lead to disaster—such as closing off whole areas of future choice.

SOME DECISIONS HAVE LENGTH TO THEM—THEY ARE TROTHS

A decision that has length to it is a troth.

A troth is a decision from which all other choosings flow. In a marriage ceremony the couple pledge their troth to each other—and within this troth a lifeful of consequences become possible.

Joining a church or synagogue should be a troth—a choice by which we can make many fruitful choices. Rightly entering into a profession requires disciplined commitment to a particular enterprise of man that flows down through the centuries as well as through the individual's life.

So fundamental is troth that no significant learning is possible without one. Nor has life any significant meaning. Decision and troth make you a center of aliveness. Make possible all other alivenesses.

The mediocrity of many people and of much education is due to the absence—or to low pressure forms—of choice, decision, commitment, sense of vocation. Combined with the assumption that rugged character comes without suffering or risk. To risk and to endure are necessary if you are to become.

TO ENDURE, TO HOLD ON, IS A NECESSARY MODE OF DECISION

Sometimes all we can do is to endure. Sometimes that is the toughest kind of decision.

The genius of being spirit is to fight battles against overwhelming odds. And perhaps not win, but play the part of a man. It is to hold on to the truth just one more day at a time, one more encounter, and so outlast and outweary hate and stupidity.

The depth of our aliveness and its disciplined toughness are evidenced by tenacity in the face of adversity. We are not distracted by "flea bites" and extraneous matters. We are resolute man. The future we see holds the present on course, memories and history feed our chosen present and future.

There are times in the life of every person when—to be man—he chooses to bear his cross. What can this possibly mean?

Having pain because we have done something wrong is not what bearing a cross means. That is only "the pains of hell" designed to bring us to repentance!

Bearing a cross is unmerited suffering which we could have avoided if we had only been willing to "go along" or "pass by on the other side"! It is meaningful suffering —enduring "for the sake of," paying the price necessary to bring good out of an evil-packed situation, meeting the reproach that comes with breaking with evil power structures that control that particular segment of the world.

There is no other way, at times, that good can be served than by the royal road of the cross. Too many people assume that a good world can be brought off without any suffering for the good on anybody's part.

RISK: DIVING INTO LIFE TWENTY FATHOMS DEEP

Life was not meant to be humdrum and closed off to adventure. We live life too cautiously. Two hundred years ago, Kierkegaard (who is one source of the viewpoint of this book) saw the staleness, lifelessness, absurdity of the life of the people of his time, in contrast with the very nature of Christianity which is to live life out of exuberance, generosity, and with a certain amount of abandon —like diving into deep water and swimming where the waves of life are heaving.

We are beginning to see that our sickness is that we repress the *good* in us. It is this, rather than the repression of our immediate pleasure impulses, that causes the deepest trouble within. The good that we would, we do not— because we are cowards.

Moments of opening out toward life, surging into life —risk—are times of aliveness. The world could stand more of this from us.

But risk is not to be confused with "kicks."

Risk is taking on a real battle, a real engagement. It is exposing one's self to possible hurt "for the sake of." Trying to bring off something new when the outcome is precarious.

Risk is *not* subjecting one's self to the roll of dice, the spin of a wheel, the chemicals of a pill or injection. All these are for the sake of kicks. They reveal the bankruptcy of real risk in one's life.

We *risk* when we deeply care about something. Risk is within a calculated decision that while we don't know the outcome, something is worth a try. "This new possibility ought to be brought off." So we act—intensely aware of our values. Risk is not yielding to momentary impulse, but is a choice.

It is the courage to invest one's life, rather than the need to prove one's courage.

DECISION MOMENTS OF A WHOLE PEOPLE

These moments of decision are not merely about private matters, nor are they always made individually. The history of a nation or a people is a series of decision moments when the road to the future is a narrow pass through mountains, and the road has to be decided for.

America is now in such a decision moment. We are in process of moving as a nation to say "yes" to a new role of the United States in earth's history. And to new possibility in white-Negro freedoms in our country. Not alone our nation but each of us personally has to choose what his life will serve in this moment of history-making. The forces and ideas of a brutal, fear-filled past, or God's creating and redeeming now?

The unforgettable symbol of such moments of decision is the assembling of the tribes of Israel by Joshua. They had escaped from Egypt, but were now wandering in the wilderness. And Joshua said to them: "Choose you this day whom you will serve. . . . But as for me and my house, we will serve the Lord." By this choice, the becoming of the Hebrews and their contribution to human civilization was once more put in motion.

THE HYPOTHESIS OF THE CHAPTER

Man greatens in decision, in troth, in acts which he intends to mean.

5

POWER TO UNDERSTAND
WHAT IS GOING ON

It's downright scary to be in a place where you are surrounded by hard-surface objects, silent, impenetrable. Where everything is an outside, and none of your senses can pierce through. Where there is no evidence of what is inside, and the center of every object around you remains inscrutable, permanently unknowable. Sometimes the whole world seems to be that way.

It's no fun to be on the outside of events—even such a simple one as three or four people talking—never quite sure what's really going on. And feeling that you never can get in on the inside.

And if you have ever had novocain put your jaw to sleep so the dentist can work on a tooth, you can sense how awful it would be if your whole body felt that way. As a something that you are a stranger to. As merely an object somehow attached to you.

You are an urge—and a necessity—to participate in life *from the inside*. And this is possible because you are a body interfused with mind. You are not shut up in a horrible surface-only world. You have the power to understand yourself and the world. You are the one form of life that can report from the inside what goes on in life.

The one source of knowledge *of* life and not merely knowledge *about* life.

Great is the function of understanding. The whole world and our whole existence is transformed for us by our power to understand.

Why do we make so little use of it, at times refuse to use it, almost trivialize it and use it for surfaces only? Why do we talk so much with the least possible exchange of understanding?

You are meant to understand the inwardness of yourself and what is going on in the world. You are a power to interpret what is happening. To figure things out and invent enterprises and gadgets. To manufacture meanings in which you live.

Actualizing this potential which is in you is a goal of life. An aliveness which is yours to nurture.

YOU ARE LIFE WHICH MUST UNDERSTAND ITSELF

You are given to yourself as something to understand.

A lifetime is all too short to bring that off. You will continue to be a puzzle to yourself. And of great interest.

Always you will be working away at understanding and trueing up the touchy energetic center of yourself—your picture of who you are and what you are made of. And being what you are, what kind of future you have—i.e., your possibility.

Your working picture of yourself comes largely as a deposit of your own experiences. Both the peak and very boring ones. So no one else can give you an identity—your own sensing of who and what you are.

But it may help to understand that as a human being, you have a core of potential which is yours to explore and develop. This core is with you wherever you go and whatever you do. And because of it, you feel guilty and unfulfilled—or good—about what you have just done and are becoming.

First of all, you are a capacity for deep feeling. Inherently you are a concern about what happens to yourself and other people. You care about persons and desperately want to be one. So it's OK to feel intensely. Make it a part of your guiding identity.

Secondly, a person is a hunger to find out "What is true to me? To what can I be true?" You have been given the privilege of partly making yourself—by your choices, decisions, troths, resoluteness. It is terribly important to understand that you are this hunger for fidelity—and how you are.

By nature you are a communal being. You are communication, coexistence, co-creation. You are designed to be with and for people—even in a very conflictful and precarious world. That you are this, and where you are this, is much of what you have to understand about yourself. And a direction of your becoming.

You are—actually now and in potential yet to be developed—an attempt to understand the world and all that is therein. You are a constant attempt to transform raw event into meanings by which you live.

You were born potential freedom. At times you can be one freedom encountering another freedom. At times you can transcend what you have been and become more than you now are. But you have to make a life out of the givens of your times and place, not in some fantasy of paradise. You—as well as every other human being—are enslaved again and again.

And the vital core of any person's identity is his sense of where he is a truth.

Together these six ideas give you creative knowledge *about* yourself. They could be summarized by saying that you are *spirited* existence. Not a thing.

But only through your own experiencings—and reflection upon these experiences until you understand them *from within*—will you gain knowledge *of* your identity.

PERSON-PERCEPTION AS UNDERSTANDING

There are other people in the world. In order to have significant relationships with anyone, you have to understand him. You can't relate to something when you haven't the faintest idea what it is.

So for centuries, power to understand others has been considered one of the distinguishing marks of a humane man. And to be understood—and to understand—is one of the exquisite joys of life.

It is the way we develop each other as persons. And become persons to each other.

So in our time, young people—and just *people*—are breaking out all over the world to know people in other countries. To understand what they make of life, what makes them tick, what can be expected of them.

There is future for one who is skilled in person-perception. Who can tune into the inwardness of another person, catch understandingly his identity as of that moment.

UNDERSTANDING WHAT IS GOING ON

The whole world is a theater of life, an inexhaustible universe for man to explore, invent and test hypotheses, try to do something with. Without resistant material we would not learn to create. Without meeting something that is clearly not his wishes and desires, man's identity is weak. So fortunately we have the world of nature to comprehend.

History-making as it occurs in a school, family, nation, world has something of this same quality. For in it we have to deal with intentions, passions, imaginations that are not ours but are of other people involved in the situation. By this we grow. So we need skill in understanding what is going on in them, how they see and interpret events, what attitudes they really take toward what is happening.

Your ability—and that of your fellow citizens—to interpret the daily news of the world becomes more important each year.

For by newspaper, television, and radio, news is not only generously but overwhelmingly available. But what does it mean? And what of it is important?

News, rather than views, determines public opinion. Or perhaps more accurately, views insinuated into news reports. News, news commentary, interpretation of the news, selection of which news to present or listen to, the manner of its presentation finally shapes a country's philosophy of life and its willingness to act.

Our saturation with daily news probably teaches us more philosophy of life than the schools do, and more about the meaning of life than the liturgy of the church gets inside us. So much so that some students of mass communications speak of "the daily liturgy of the news." By that they mean that newspapers and electronic news reports are constant celebration of the recurring dark passions of man, his brutalities, explosions of the irrational, stinking sordidness, impotent goodness. This is the *profane* liturgy of man's daily news. It is the news that is profitable to broadcast. And it probably produces in the listener a mind that hungers to repeatedly saturate itself with such a liturgy.

Within the events of a single day of the world there is also a sacred liturgy. A celebration of the struggle "just folks" put up against almost overwhelming odds, of the cry for justice, of the continuing postponement, for at least one more day, of total destruction, of the breaking down of walls into a world-circling communication. We can read the news as the awesome liturgy which mankind offers each day of that day's toil and suffering to God and fellow man toward an unknowable future.

Who is able to so interpret the flood of news each day? Who is willing to become able to make the good try at it? Who can sense the weather in the storms of history-making?

This is the world you are living in and helping to shape. You are to nurture and discipline your potential to understand and interpret news and world events.

45

A THREAT WHICH YOU MUST HELP TO RESIST

There is a crippling of the human mind which many people—consciously and unconsciously—are accomplishing today.

The years of the twentieth century have been distinguished by vast efforts to eliminate, warp, and sicken the great words of civilization.

Man has been misled by propaganda staged on national and world scale. He has been forced to believe the propaganda—at least to act as if he did. The great words are misused to mean anything the party wants them to mean. Terroristic rulership is called "people's democracy"; war is called "peace-loving"; God is announced as dead; sexual exploitation of others is called love; maintaining a priviledged place at the top of the totem pole is liberty and justice for all.

All the "fast buck boys" are out to capture the market —and therefore the mind—of the listener. Their name is legion. Their frequent route is to sell shoddy meanings of life in order to sell their product. And to reduce people to nervously moving from one thing to another in a world of noise and fleeting emotion.

The common effort in all propaganda is an attempt to destroy the habit of truthfully thinking by substituting the "feelies" of Huxley's *Brave New World*. To create mass mind.

At their worst, political propagandists of the radical right and left try to destroy our trust in each other, fragment our nation, isolate little pockets of victims which they can attack with impunity. For facts and thoughtful consideration they substitute noise, ridicule, vicious attack upon persons' reputations.

They are destroying the very foundations of mind which make a thinking, humane man possible.

One of the great civilizing enterprises in the years ahead is to resist this effort and to defeat it on a community, national, and world scale. Where are you in that battle for the foundations of mind? And how well equipped?

BUT WHAT IS THE PROCESS OF UNDERSTANDING?

It's very hard to describe how we go about understanding. But let me try, and you take it on from there. What has to happen if we are to understand something?

Basically, "understanding" means "standing in." Standing along with the person in his situation. Walking around, seeing and feeling it from the inside—the way he is feeling and seeing it. And therefore knowing what is *moving within* the person and situation. You are no longer on the outside looking at the surface.

Which is why we can really know only that which we deeply love, and deeply love only that whose nature we understand.

Both love and understanding involve a respectful *tuning in* to the other's deep feeling. Both involve seeing how he sees the situation he is in. Both are founded on sensitivity. Unless you can comprehend the existence situation of another person *as he experiences it,* you have no original data for either understanding or love.

But to understand is more yet. To understand is to make sense out of what you see and feel and of contemporary happenings in the world. It is to transform happenings into meaningful world.

Making sense involves being able to symbolize what is going on—to put it into words. You have to find a word, a phrase, a sentence which presents to you what is going on. (The word can also re-present to you what went on, so that you can keep on exploring the situation and thinking about it at other times). The word helps because it connects with other words whose meaning you already comprehend.

So to understand well requires that you have a good supply of words with which to do the symbolizing. Not just any words, but words that call up vivid experiences you have had, or events that have happened in other people's lives.

But a word cannot call up vivid experiencings unless you have had them. So you have to have a rich supply of firsthand experiencing if you are to understand anything well. You must have gone places and done things. Been in the thick of things happening. And then be able to connect your experiences with the great words. It is for this richness of power to symbolize that you go after an education, read books and articles, talk with people who have ideas.

You don't need to know a great many ideas. By this time you have learned that if you understand well the few key words in a book or a teacher's lecture—*and can use them*—you are "in." Actually you are probably suffering indigestion from the number of thoughts and opinions hurled at you all your life by magazines, television, books, schools. Strip your mind down to a few elemental great ideas and understand them *well*. With their help, possess *your* experiences. Do you know the great words of your civilization in this way?

A pip-squeak mind and personality can't understand anybody—not even itself.

6

BEING WITH AND FOR PEOPLE

Being with and for persons is much of a full life. It's a way of becoming alive. And keeping alive. The greatness of a person is measured by his power to be with and for people.

"WITH" DOES NOT MEAN TO BE A SHEEP

Being with and for people does not mean agreeing with their ideas and actions, nor going along with the crowd or being lost in the herd. What it does mean is that fundamentally you are for others—as persons.

Actually any relationship is shaky until it has proved itself able to exist in spite of differences. And a friendship is productive only when each is an integrity—with experiences, thoughts, areas of expertness which each brings to the relationship. Sheep do not live *with* or *for*: they live merely as crowd and run as crowd.

Some of the worst disasters to mankind in our century have come because people allowed themselves to be forced to live as sheep. The teen-age culture of a school or community can have this disease. By adulthood it can become a way of life.

With does not mean "always being around people." It is not defined by geography. Some of the most horrible "non-withness" is of people in the same house, office, city. As used here, *with* is a personal, psychological, philosophical, religious term.

To emphasize this different meaning, we will always use *with* in this chapter italicized.

The proper meaning of *with* is carried by these phrases —common fate, tuned in, co-create.

WE ARE IN A COMMON FATE

"Being *with*" comes from common fate rather than from trying to be copies of each other.

Common fate means that we're both in the same battle, neither of us will win—or survive—without the other, the peculiar talents of each are needed, and each knows that when the going gets tough the other will not chicken out and run.

Common fate behavior is the objective basis—and test —of whether a relationship is friendship and love or something merely having the appearance of the real thing.

As long as everything is going well or life is one exciting pleasure after another, anyone can collect numbers of fair-weather friends. When the chips are down and the battle may be lost or a long hard pull is ahead, then you discover that they were in love with *their* feeling excitement when around you, rather than in love with *you*. They really didn't *care* for you, but only for you as satellite for their projects and emotions.

Finally—and always—the basis of human relationships is basic trust. And you never know the real article until you go through a common fate struggle together. In fact, it never becomes the real article until you go through a common fate. Before that it is only a possibility. Afterward it is a confident expectancy—life filled with faith, hope, love.

Common fate behavior testifies that all involved see each other as *fellow* man. We can disagree with each other; each can have his uniqueness; there are differences and distances; we may not even like everything about the other. But we are bound together in the bundle of life. We are *with* each other.

Common fate kind of *with* is very solid and realistic. It is much more than mere emotion about each other. And it takes courage. Often it is a choosing to be *with* when others are leaving. It is the comradeship of a society of justice, of fighting a common enemy, of together causing something to happen.

You will never know very many of the people of your country, nor really like all that you meet. But you can live with a high sense of being caught up with them in a common fate and destiny. Then you will not be limited to associating with only the people who wear the same kind of clothes that you do, can pay for the same kind of house and automobile, think the same kind of opinions that you treasure.

A merely mutual admiration society is not friendship. For what happens if either no longer pleases at the moment? What happens when the world has to be encountered? When new events come over the horizon? Nor does *withness* exist in a society of conformists, i.e., in a sheep culture. Unfortunately, in most gangs and in-groups the members are living out of dependency and fear.

Anyone who has ever been a crucial member of an athletic team, or played in an orchestra, or been part of a group bringing an organization to life, or demonstrating and fighting for a cause knows the thrill and bindingness of common fate.

TUNED IN

With has also another quality. You are tuned in to each other. You are in resonance rather than merely being alongside or coming in as noise.

What is meant by being tuned in can be felt better than defined. It's hard to say exactly what it is. It's more than merely liking the same persons and the same things. Although it is that, and may begin there.

You are no longer strangers to each other. You are not wooden and alien stuff to each other, speaking a different language, broadcasting on a totally different wave length. You hear more than static and noise. You make sense to each other. You feel at home with each other. This is more than being tuned in on the dance floor. The tuning in is to each other, and not just reaction to a beat and throb coming in from some ready-made world. Some people mistake this latter for the central tuning.

The central tuning is this: you are tuned in to "where each other lives"—that core within each of you which you keep hidden from most people, and which finally is your integrity. You know some of both the good and the bad in each other, for you have been through many different kinds of experiences together. You have some inkling of each other's life goals. Once in awhile each of you speaks out of conviction. You feel each other's defeats and triumphs. When the other suffers, you suffer with him.

Being tuned into another person can be vividly understood by thinking of its opposite—how it feels to be estranged. How it is to be not only out of touch with another, but to feel the other as alien. As strange stuff coming from a totally different world. As something you can't participate in even when you try.

AUTHENTIC INTIMACY

Intimacy is another word for *with*.

There is much spurious intimacy being foisted upon people today. Alcoholic hilarity is not necessarily intimacy. Nor is a flushed body. Sex relations without being tuned in to where each other is living, without previous history of sharing ideas, life goals, and fidelity to each other's growth, are both spurious and destructive—even if inside marriage, where sex relations properly belong. The "life of the party" is not necessarily really *with* anybody but may be trying to escape from his sense of weakness in intimacy. Calling each other by first name does not necessarily mean that we see each other as unique and treasured individuality.

With means that you are aware of the other as a struggling human being trying to make his way in a precarious world. To you, he is a *spirited* existence. And you are a presence to him.

You are permeable to each other. You get through to the other person. And there is room in the purposes of one for the other's feelings, room in his imagination for the new possibility exploding in the other's mind, room in his life project for the other person's life enterprise.

You have both entered each other far enough that you are aware of the depth, rather than just the surface each presents. And you genuinely respect what you have found. Not only respect, but are a good friend of its growth and development. The mature form of intimacy is this creative fidelity to each other's growth—come hell or high water.

Creative fidelity is what is meant by *for*.

If the prevailing style of your relationship to people is to use them for your purposes, manipulate them, regard them as mere footnotes in your biography, to live *alongside* them rather than *with* them, then the world finally becomes a very cold place, and a cosmic chill of loneliness creeps inside you.

A truly religious faith enables being *with* and *for* people. Not just because our religious heritage teaches us that we *should* love other people—although it does. But because we feel the love and creativeness of God coming toward us in power. And welling up within us toward our fellow man, convincing us that God is just as concerned about their lives as he is about ours.

The vital moments of religious history have been such outbreakings. The damnable periods have been those either of lethargic love or violent hatred of all those not of the faith, culminating in wars of religions, fanatical persecution, withdrawal of love from the men of the world into a constricted pool of ever-evaporating relationship.

Your generation is called to be out-flowing—breaking down barriers, breaking out of ghettoes all over the world.

To be *with* and *for* man wherever he is. "I was not born to share in hatred, but to share in love" is the cry of your generation.

You are to nurture this potential and this common fate.

CO-CREATE: EACH OTHER AND AN ENTERPRISE

To be *with* and *for* people means to co-create, not just to have sympathy for them or like them.

First of all, we can (and do) co-create each other.

A mysterious event often goes on between people. Like a candle causing another to burst into flame on a dark night, we bring each other alive. Often this happens merely upon a person's coming into the room. Even before a word is said, faces light up. Or to change the metaphor, alone by yourself, you were a Dead Sea. Someone comes, and all kinds of life begin to take shape, flutter and swim. Just this person's presence creates you as an aliveness.

People can have this effect on each other. They can also snuff out the flame already there or dampen it so that it smolders.

Whatever is involved, this "lifing or deathing" is going on all the time. It is the first and basic evidence of co-creation.

A second evidence comes when we accept others as collaborators in thinking, feeling, inventing. Conversation, for instance, can be exhilarating. What one says stirs up something new in the other. That communicated in turn awakens more in the first, until by the end they have created something neither would have done alone. They are both more than when they started.

The dialectic play of mind upon mind is one of the rare and exciting joys of life.

Why don't we have more of it? Because we are accustomed to prattle? Because most conversations are monologue rather than dialogue? Because most people think there's something wrong with having ideas or being original? Because we don't trust each other and so only express our surface, don't let what we really think and feel get out? Because no one has ever told us that communication is what makes both mind (our mind!) and society?

In co-creation some aliveness in us encounters the aliveness of another with an invitation for something greater than either of us to emerge.

Good "group think" is co-creation. Inventing and carrying out an enterprise can be successful only if there is co-creation rather than domination. The problems of our time are so complex and far-reaching that only a team skilled in teaming up their minds and special abilities can match them.

In the co-creation of a new human life through mating, manhood and womanhood are *realized*. The birth to a couple of their first child is always memorable. For they have shared with the Creator in creating new life capable of creating more new life. They know at first hand tremendous Mystery and Holiness. They genuinely love.

You were meant to be *with* people. Your education and your journey through life should widen and deepen the number of people you can be *with*. Rather than the other way around—getting more narrow and exclusive.

With, for, co-create, are small words out of which great aliveness comes.

7

FREEDOM

Freedom is spontaneity—freshly doing what is relevant in a situation even though you have never done it before. And doing it with a sort of effortless style. Gracefully. Freedom is a fully functioning mind and heart able to do well what you really want to do.

Freedom is a sense that you are all together in one piece—not torn apart nor in dead center in such conflict that you are unable to move.

Freedom is to be an *I* rathar than an *it*, a subject rather than just an object. An agent and not a patient of civilization.

Freedom is a sense that you are participating warmly in humanity and are in touch with the sources of life for all people.

EXPRESSIVE RATHER THAN REACTIVE LIVING

Nothing a human does is *natural*. *Human* action comes with the conviction "*I am*, and I intend my acts to be an expression of *me* and not just of the chemistry of nature."

So freedom begins in a person when he can say "I." Not just as a repetition of a sound he hears but as an act of self-awareness.

Aware of himself and thinking "I," he can stand off from what is going on and take an *attitude toward* what is happening. And toward himself. Freedom becomes possible.

Saying "I," he is no longer bound to the determinisms of raw nature. He is no longer just a creature of nature, he is *man* who lives in a cultural world—i.e., nature interfused with meanings and spirit. Accordingly, there's nothing more stupid or menacing than the argument we're often given that we should do something because "It's natural!" Everything a *man* does is *nature interfused with culture*, with meanings.

Every human act is *speech*—something said about self, about others, about the meaning of life.

Every act is a language. A nonverbal communication to the world. Some of your behavior says, "The meaning of life is to protect and defend myself." The message of other things you do is, "The goal of life is to be eternal suckling," or, "You made me what I am today, I hope you're satisfied." Or, "I should have the world as I want it, on my own terms, and now." These particular *act speeches* are expressions of unfreedom.

Man as freedom declares, "I am not an empty receiver of sensations, or a blank page upon which anybody can write anything he wants, or a dummy whose speech is supplied by either raw nature or the most clever ventriloquist who makes noises in my ear. My spoken words—verbal or actions—are *my* words. They are neither anonymous nor somebody else's. *I* am."

AFFIRM RESPONSIBLE SELF

A person takes another step into freedom when he begins to take responsibility for what he does, when he says, "I did that; I hold myself responsible."

This does not mean, "I *alone* did that. I brought it off all by myself." It does mean, "I assented; I chose; I gave in; I was an *agent* in this event."

Recovery from "sick, sick, sick" is impossible until the person begins to experience himself as responsible agent. Until he affirms that he participated in bringing about the trouble and can participate in its healing. This recognition moment—vividly felt—is the beginning of new life. For by this very recognition he has *transcended what he was* in the act. He has projected himself beyond it. He is in the realm of freedom.

Further, we become responsible characters as others *treat us as* responsible people. Deal with us as if we were grown up, could be trusted, would thrive on being given an important job to do and take the consequences.

IN THE RESPONSIBLE LIFE, GUILT IS REAL AND IS WORKED THROUGH

We know now that if we *are* guilty, we should feel guilty.

Excusing ourselves (and others) for what has happened is no help to anyone. Nor is letting ourselves and others evade the necessary *guilt work* that must follow when we are guilty. To violate another human dignity, to be insensitive to another's need or joy, to refuse to become manifest and exist in power are serious matters. They must be faced and worked through.

We must learn how to travel this road from infancy to maturity.

This freeing process of working through guilt is quite different from having a *biting* conscience that keeps constantly telling us, "You have not done what I told you to do." A biting, tearing conscience is demonic fury destroying our freedom. It is one of the reasons for the cautiousness with which so-called good people live. "I have measured out my life with coffee spoons." To do that certainly is not freedom.

HEALTHY CONSCIENCE IS A NECESSITY FOR FREEDOM

What then is a good conscience? For without a healthy conscience you do not live in freedom.

Conscience is yourself deeply caring about others and yourself. Conscience is a governance system whose powers come from that caring. Conscience is yourself as private detective, plaintiff, judge. As historian. As coach and developer.

You are not "in freedom" unless you can transcend what happens and what you now are in the situations of life. Otherwise there is no chance for becoming. You would be stuck with a senseless repetition of what you have been and total determination by the outside world. You would be shut up in the world of "the natural." You would not be free spirit.

In all these conscience actions, you are fundamentally a

good friend of yourself. Your conscience is not saying to you, "O *enemy*, I have found you out."

Conscience does prick you, cause you to feel bad, sometimes sends you into the depths of despair about yourself. But health and freedom come from going on through rather than trying to evade or postpone conscience work. "Let not the sun go down on your wrath" is wisdom.

Conscience is not primarily for the sake of accusing you. It calls you to see *realistically and truthfully* what is and what now can be. It enables you to recognize *both* the good and the evil.

Only the biting conscience thunders, "This miserable thing that you have done—that is all you are." Biting conscience has two favorite weapons—concentration on some one disastrous moment and a constant focus of your attention upon a drooping image of yourself. These two acts raise up a dark menacing mountain, shutting off all horizon. So you can no longer live with expectancy—except of disaster. Hope is no more.

What happens in healthy conscience work? You do feel deeply the awfulness of what has happened. But you are not just overcome by emotion. You truthfully see what is in the situation. "So it happened. What now is the possibility that can be called out of the situation?" You begin to be real and take off the mask.

As you begin to move, rather than sit around in your guilt feelings, you may discover that there is a healing and creating going on in the world of persons not altogether of your own making. And nothing you do can cut you off from the possibility of freshly participating in it.

Talking with someone who genuinely cares for you is

often a beginning step in such healing. For such talk is forgiveness coming toward you from the community of man which you have wronged. So it is a beginning escape from your shut-up-ness.

So far we have dealt with conscience as if it operated only when you did something wrong or failed to do something. If the concept of conscience as *"ourselves as freedom"* is correct, then conscience is equally functioning when you see something better that can become real, and become totally absorbed in it.

In recall from ill or call to good, conscience is a call to *become*. To become authentic. Conscience is potential pushing us to actualize it. To become what we can be. To fully function as a center of aliveness.

So a healthy conscience directs our attention both backward and forward. But it is even more concerned with the future and present than with the past.

FREE SPIRIT IS CREATIVE

At the very center of freedom is creativity—the emergence of genuine novelty from the self-in-world which we are.

Great origination of service to all mankind happens only in a few. But these few came out of an age or time that made possible their creative acts. Often there was such general ferment and crisis that, if that particular person hadn't originated, someone else would have. In all cases they invented on from what other men had done.

Television, for instance, was not possible until after several original thinkers each had his explosive "aha" of pure thought about the nature of the universe.

Each of us, in his own here and now, is invited to be this freedom in whatever ways are possible for him.

A climate can exist in a school which awakens and empowers origination in its students. And school is then exciting and memorable. A true habitat of the human spirit. Or it can be a quite different—and alarming—climate. Over in the city of Athens, a whole climate for a few brief years stimulated men into an exuberance of creating in many fields.

You can establish a group of friends—one other, five others, or forty—which creates you as *functioning* mind and heart. Within such a group you will experience yourself as freedom. As spirit originating and creating. But you must help bring off such a group, not ask that it be handed to you.

Also you can depend on your own mind to create—if you are willing to be a good friend of it.

You can depend upon your mind to come up with fresh ideas and invention about things you are concerned about—if only you will invite it, feed it, and give it one uncluttered hour each day to work. Preferably the first hour in the morning before you are stultified by the commonplace or by distracting electronic noises beamed toward mass mind. Let your mind become totally absorbed in something for a period of time, pursue a new idea as it will. Each day and over a period of time.

COURAGE TO BECOME MANIFEST

Finally, freedom is the courage to become manifest in the world. To stand up so that you can be counted in the life of your group.

The unfree person is ruled by fear. Fear that he may make a mistake. Fear he may be ridiculed, ostracized, cut off from human warmth. Fear that others find out what a despicable person he really is on the inside. Until no one is himself, but tries to be everybody else.

So spirit sickens and dies. Openness and trust between persons is only pretended. Origination—except in unimportant matters—is no more. Heart quits pulsing. And the smell of death comes through the mask of gracious living.

Give us to be men who will not be swayed by prevalent winds of opinion and prejudice, but can say to them with authority, "Peace, be still." Give us to be elemental characters who are manifest and free as the as yet untamed mountains and clouds and as originating as the tiny seed in the mantle of earth.

How significant do you regard freedom to be?

8

BEING A TRUTH

No one can be a center of self-propelling aliveness who is not a truth. Becoming the truth you were meant to be is another life-long enterprise.

YOU ARE TO BE A TRUTH

You are meant to be a truth. To be authentic. The real article and not a phony.

The most fundamental kind of truth is not a *statement* which corresponds to fact but a *person who is an integrity*.

If you are that kind of truth, all other truths are possible. Without it, really nothing is possible. Nothing. Except disaster.

Socrates was a truth. Jesus was a truth. Science today is not primarily the findings of science and its uses, but the world community of scientists, extending through time, each disciplined in a tested way of thinking and experimenting, and in truthful communication with the rest of the community. So no one listens to a scientist who is caught not being an integrity in his profession.

In no area of life do we trust traitors and hypocrites—people whose behavior does not coincide with the good words they use. Who try to put up a front and convince the rest of us that the front is what they really are. Who talk out of both sides of their mouths, are quick-change artists like chameleons, live lives of duplicity driven by fear that they will be found out. And they are found out—they become known for the absence in them of sincere workings of mind and heart.

More importantly, not to be a truth is living death.

CENTEREDNESS AND SIGNIFICANT SHAPE

Scattered excitements and furor about everything is not aliveness.

We have to clarify what we really want out of life. Become *significant* form—not just any shape.

As with all works of art, we have to cease being a mess. Enthusiasm has to take on characteristic style and march through time, collecting more energies as it goes. Aliveness requires a centeredness which can bring all sorts of experiences together so that they explode into futures. Effective thrust into life can come only from a mobilized center.

So we have to become something *in particular*. Cease being diffused, *mean something*.

Unfortunately many people remain nebulous clouds all their lives. They would be hard put to discover any organizing truth that gives design and significance to their lives. Their shape is determined from the outside by the environment. And by their desire to get ahead and have pleasure in it. Neither of these is being a truth.

You are meant to be a powerful truth. Significant centeredness.

MEANINGFUL INTEGRITY

A person can be an integrity about very stupid and unimportant matters. Many of us are! So find something significant and meaningful as the organizer of your integrity.

How can you find something so big that it is involved in all situations and therefore usable wherever you are? And so vital that it pulls you in the direction of life rather than toward nothingness or demonry?

I believe it might be the idea of the Kingdom of God. For the Kingdom of God speaks of new possibility beyond what now is. Though it is even now in our midst, it is "not yet." But it is possibility whose time has come. It is New Time emerging from Old Time—breaking out in power at particular points in the more personal situations of our life and in this moment of history-making. A new humanity is struggling to be born in civilization through the travail of good and evil in our time. It is present as horizon and new life in every situation you face.

This new possibility, this new aliveness, you must try to discover. And throw your energies into it with a certain amount of reckless abandon.

For you can know this kind of truth only to the degree that you take part in it. So that the ocean is in the fish and the fish is in the ocean. A spectator, a sitter on the sidelines, a looker-on, an uninvolved person who is not trying to actualize it in his own life will never know this truth. Reading in newspapers, magazines, books, about the struggle for justice, quoting the Bible on justice, is not enough. *You* are to be embodied truth. That is the only kind there is. And the only way life becomes meaningful.

Your life *means* when you begin to function as part of something more important than yourself, when you find your place in a larger scheme. The worth and intensity of your life depends upon how significant that larger system is.

A man faithful only to himself would find life absurd. Meaning would happen when he saw some significant world and an opening in it for his life.

Meaning happens when our lives become tendoned on to something greater than ourselves. When an opening is offered us in which we and the things we care for can expand and become real.

AN INTEGRITY THROUGH A LENGTH OF TIME

Being a truth means to be an integrity over a period of time. A continuing integrity that flexibly devises plans as it goes along. That develops—and not merely changes as it goes. Meaningful integrity has a time dimension. Another name for it is creative fidelity.

While a person of integrity is always open to transformation, this is not the same as flip-flop when under pressure. Integrity is to march together with *truth*. And to do so is the only kind of peace we can find in this world.

This involves putting together a directional walk that combines past-present-future into some meaningful story. Utterly disjointed life is absurd, meaningless, has no becoming. It has no "task, plan, and freedom to carry it out." And that no-ness is person sickness.

For man lives as time, not just *in* time. Each New Year's Day we rightly speak of "Father" Time.

As human beings, we live right now a *future-past-present all put together*.

We can't live *in* the past. Those battles in the particular occasions when they happened, we do not risk. The people who lived then did that. We have to face our decisions and crises.

And since we are creatures of memory and imagination, we can't live each present as if it had no connections with past identity or with possibility into futures. Nor can we live now in the future—for things will be different when chronological future actually arrives. But we can live now *toward* a future. In every meaningful moment, we are an awareness of a future-past-present. Which we now live.

You are destined to live life this way whether you want to or not!

Those who think they are meaningful integrity when they live only momentary fragments—only in each present —are kidding themselves and trying to kid the world.

You can try to drown your sorrows and resentments. You can try to drug your consciousness so that it escapes into fanciful worlds. But always your mind as a time-binder asserts itself. Your mind is forever busy weaving together what is now happening, your stock of memories, and the futures it imagines. Short of death, you can't stop this process. You can impoverish it and try to play games with it.

But a *story* of your life will come up in your consciousness.

"BE A TRUTH" MEANS BECOMING A TRUTH

You are always *becoming* a truth. No person is a finished or perfected truth. It is very important that he know this fact about himself.

For actually every human truth is a mixture of good and not so good. You can always find faults in every person's character and many mistakes in his living. It cannot be required of any man (or child!) that he be perfect and never make mistakes. But he is subject to two criteria. Is he free to see and recognize his mistakes for what they are and do something about them? Over the long haul, is he fundamentally making the good try to march together with significant *truth*?

For instance, David of Old Testament days was a pretty horrible man at times, but he became a truth to many people because he did come to terms with these two criteria.

The person who has come up the hard way, who has fought battles and temptations but has learned courage and how to recover, finally is more able to help the rest of us than one who has never struggled.

LIFE AS HERO JOURNEY

In the image of life as a hero journey, we can now bring to focus all that we have been developing about being a truth. Hang this picture in your mind for reference and tenacity in the face of adversity.

Being a truth means journeying down an often lonesome valley toward a goal that sometimes almost disappears. Fighting battles and demons. Getting bloodied and beat.

But holding the center until you have won some pioneering truth for that part of the world in which you live.

This is the only way you grow up and mature.

Your one life on earth is to be a journey through chronological time by yourself as meaningful time. Being a truth involves moving together with *truth* over a period of time.

So you are set up to be a hero journey. By "hero," we do not mean someone who is in the spotlight, wildly acclaimed by shrieks and yells, but someone who has *journeyed*. And has won from his battles a good for his fellow man.

The myths of almost all peoples picture such a journey for the young person who wants to become adult.

According to this universal myth, the beginning of growing up (of being no longer a child) is to go on a journey of your own, leaving—when necessary—the support of friends and familiar community. Find yourself in a situation where you have to depend on what you can do; nobody's going to rescue you. You have to stand up and bring off the enterprise.

You meet the demons that try to destroy man—hatred and brutality and stupidities which are quite real in the world. You battle them. Within you, giants of despair get at you. The lonely ghost of "nobody here" begins to disintegrate you. But somehow you hang on and win to the castle—often helped by whispered wisdom.

Out of the battling comes the discovery that the youth is the King's son. The young person discovers the Eternal Father and is given a destiny. He is joined in marriage to

Love, to live ever after with Love in a transformed Kingdom.

With these hard-won secrets of life—so the myth goes —he returns to his people to make offering of this new mode of life. To his surprise, he is laughed at and treated as an unwelcome upstart. But if he can "take it" and remain true to his journey, the Kingdom stirs.

Notice that everything depended on his *courage in the first place to leave the community of "they"*—where nobody thinks, but lives by fashion and custom; where nobody really is, but only crowd is; where the dead hand of the past is constantly burying the present and the future; where pleasure rather than *suffering for the becoming good* is the rule of life.

Even so, Abraham went out, not knowing where he was going, but looking for a city "whose builder and maker is God." Even so, Moses "forsook Egypt, not fearing the wrath of the king: for he endured, as seeing him who is invisible."

The truth you were meant to be is such a lifelong pilgrimage. Pioneering. Fighting battles. Making the good try to be integrity, an agent of meaning to other people.

Section III

BRINGING OFF
LIFE WORLDS

9

YOUR ALIVENESS CENTERS A WORLD

WHAT WE HAVE DONE SO FAR

In the section of the book which we have just completed, we have explored six goals for you as a center of aliveness —caring and feeling deeply, decision and troth, power to understand and so live life from the inside, being with and for people, being a freedom, and the truth you were meant to be.

This is a picture of what your potential really is. You can count on these alivenesses' trying to actualize themselves. They will push you toward becoming a person. They're *for* you over a period of time.

Also you now know what you are to be a good friend of in other people—these six alivenesses.

BRINGING OFF A LIFE WORLD

In this new section we move into bringing off a life world. We talked about this in the first chapter in a beginning way—now we will try to really develop it.

We are born into a great system of giving and receiving. To take part in it—even unwillingly—is the only way we live.

We "breathe" the whole world about us. And something of us takes up its residence in other people. Our person extends beyond our skin. We cannot be located merely in our body or its geographical location. Even when we are not geographically present, we may be present in people's minds and in their becoming. By writing a letter we can influence what happens a thousand miles away. We can be present in other people's memories and hopes for the future even when we are far distant in time.

We permeate each other; we are present in each other. We influence and form each other's personality. We exude feelings and actions which help determine the feeling tone of our home, our class at school, the other person with whom we are talking. We are constantly offering good or not-so-good possibilities to some situation. Each moment we are selecting out what we will pay attention to. What giving-receiving we will initiate with the persons and objects we have selected. Which people and events are foreground; which are background and fringe. In each here and now we are constantly helping to organize "a world" in which we and others exist. The flavor and energy of our offerings significantly affect the kind of little world that results.

You cannot live as an isolated self, feeding on just yourself with energies turned back in on yourself. With nothing going out or coming in. With no organization by you of worlds in which you carry on transactions. You can live only as self-in-world.

You can willingly take part in such life by a whole-hearted giving and receiving. Or you can pretend that this isn't the way life is and be mediocre all your life. It is best to intend a life world. Say yes to this way that life functions. Be a large enough mind and heart to fill the special worlds you inhabit with feeling and help determine their development.

So now we look at the kind of life world you intend to co-create with other people and all the other energies of the universe.

Each chapter will deal with just one staging area of your giving and receiving, becoming and dying, in this earth. I have chosen to deal with your possible world of fellow man, with the new human consciousness and the public opinion in which you will live, with the larger history-making you will be a part of, with family, work, leisure time. Each of these staging areas is part of the whole territory which your life inhabits.

We will have to use the term "life world" for the whole territory which includes them all, and also for each particular staging area. This double use of the same word may cause some confusion, but the essential meaning of the phrase does apply to both.

For life world is what actually is transacting with you in a particular lived moment. In this particular here and now, you have selected out and helped organize a "little world." For example, your life world of public opinion is not such a vague generality as the whole world of public opinion, but that portion of public opinion in which you are *present as a concerned enterprise.* Which you are helping form, and is forming you.

Life world also means the fairly stable world which you inhabit. Again it is not the whole universe, but the arena of *your* life. The territory which is your habitat. The place where life-or-death-for-me transactions take place.

Where many particular occasions of momentary life world are staged.

Your life world is also *your style* of taking part in giving and receiving, in creating and consuming, your *mode* of being-in-the-world.

The next few chapters now try to lay out some important possibilities of each of the six life worlds that you must put together into a one living system which is you-in-this-world.

If you have ever looked at an anatomy booklet that was a series of transparent overlays, each page giving only one part of the total working body—one page is the body as surface contours and skin; another overlay page is the body as flesh; other pages to lay on top of each other are the body as muscle system, the body as skeleton, the body as blood system, as nerve system—you will know how to use these chapters. Put them all on top of each other, and you can see yourself and the life world in which you now can start functioning.

Here is life as a wholeness and as a depth, in some of its dimensions and possible influence. That world of situations, actions, persons which will constitute life for you.

10

A HABITAT FOR YOURSELF
COMPOSED OF FELLOW MEN

We have already looked at aliveness as power to live with people. Now we move to considering what is involved in bringing off a habitat composed of fellow men.

So we have to get clear—what is a fellow man?

FELLOW MAN

Fellow man is one who is co-creator and co-manager of your particular life world in some time and place. And you feel comfortable with him in that role.

What makes him fellow man is that you believe in him. And he believes in you.

It is very difficult to say just what "to believe in somebody" involves. It is more than trust, though certainly trust is in it. When we believe in someone, we have a conviction that we understand what kind of human material he is and what he basically intends—even in the temporary absence of evidence. Or even with evidence that he is off on a detour. Belief in a person requires some *idea of what that person is.* Belief is a reasoned conviction about him—particularly about his long-term potential—that carries us through dry spells and times of tension.

The heart of believing in a person is that *you both know that both of you believe in something significant other than just yourselves*. Being fellow man consists not just of looking at each other, but looking together at important reality. Love is not gazing at each other's eyes, but also being totally absorbed in something significant beyond either person. You are held together within significant symbol, i.e., held together by some common understanding and response to that which you are looking at. Thus you are not totally victimized by immediate conflicts involving each other.

A convictional belief in a person also comes about because you have stood within each other long enough that you now know each other. You do not feel the other as alien stuff. The other is credible. Believable. You understand him and can make sense out of him. Not completely, but enough to relate to him. You don't just have pity on him or sympathize with him. You see him as co-creator.

You experience each other as freedom. When together, you are one freedom invoking another freedom. You are friends of each other's growth and functional autonomy. Neither person is merely satellite to the other. While your lives and awarenesses overlap, they are not identical. Both of you are centers of aliveness and unique integrity. There are healthy distances and unoccupied openings in the togetherness.

But your fates and destinies converge enough that you recognize that you are walking trails in the same direction. So some walking together is possible. And the same enemy menaces both of you.

These five realities constitute fellow man. They are what Abou ben Adam should have meant when he asked to be put down as "one who loves his fellow men." Being a friend to *fellow* men is more than living "in a house by the side of the road." When we speak of bringing off a life world of fellow man, the image is of a current of many streams flowing together, each influencing the other and together exerting great power. We are not talking about just picking up wounded travelers at the side of the road. And when we say fellow man, we don't mean *dual* existence—two or more total separatenesses who bump into each other, even serve and communicate *to* each other but never experience communion or create a common world.

LIFE WORLD OF DYAD—I-THOU

The simplest, deepest, most difficult life world of fellow man consists of just two people. It can be called a dyad —or meaningfully, I-Thou.

The attitude of man is twofold, in accordance with the twofold nature of the primary words which he speaks.

The primary words are not isolated words, but combined words.

The one primary word is the combination *I-Thou*.

The other primary word is the combination *I-It*.[1]

The meaning here is really quite difficult, for so much

[1] Martin Buber, *I and Thou* (Charles Scribner's Sons, New York, 1958), p. 3.

is packed into so few words. So let's take some time on it. For it is a basic text.

One thing that is being said is this: Contrary to popular belief, we do not exist as just *ourselves*. We exist only as part of a world—in combination with something. There is no such thing as a self; only self-in-world. There is no life without the hyphen!

To be human being we "hyphen" with other human beings.

Our basic relationship with a *human* being has to be a different quality and style than our relationship to an "it"—else we too become impersonal. For what the hyphen connects us to influences the quality of our "I." And likewise the nature of the hyphen. The Buber quotation suggests how crucial it is that your world be I-Thou.

But what is a Thou? A Thou is a *presence*. If you have ever sensed another *person* as a presence, you can understand what is meant. If you haven't, we can point to a sensitive exploration that you can make.

Right here and now a *person* is encountering you. Before you is a spirited existence, an embodied self. Something to be understood, rather than just used. A human dignity to be respected. Something that you can dialogue with. It is not a stone or a piece of wood or an *object*. It is a *subject*—which means that it is not its apparent surfaces nor the sensations it gives you. It is not your ideas of it. It is a complex of the alivenesses we have already considered.

A *person* is always *mystery*—something you will never fully understand. A person is depth, moreness. Always lurking in a person is the flash of spontaneity (which is another word for freedom). Spontaneity can never be conditioned to always buy what you want to sell, or respond as others want it to.

This sounds like an exciting kind of life world to bring off! Why are we so lethargic and stupid about it?

And we are just that. Buber brooded over the horrible way Western man went wrong in the twentieth century. It dawned in his mind that the basic mistake was stupidity in regard to the I-Thou nature of man. And venomous hostility toward it. Western man (perhaps all men) had chosen to deal with others as "its," and opted for an I-It world. He had chosen wars, dehumanized industry and science, invented styles of communication organized to destroy the foundations of mind and personality.

Buber was clear that we do have to have "I-It" in our life world. We do have to use, fashion, manipulate the things of the world—including, in some measure, people. But if we have *only* I-It, then we are in hell. I-Thou must finally govern and color our life world. Else we too become but machines and clods.

I-Thou then is the basic in bringing off a world of fellow men. Such a creative "twosomeness" may be called a dyad.

A dyad is not something that just one individual *creates*. If so, it would be only an I-It world. I-Thou life world is a co-creation. We invoke, rather than compel, the other to be present as a Thou. We *offer* (rather than *force* upon situations) whatever aliveness we may have. For we see others and deal with them as fellow men.

NUCLEAR GROUP

Beyond the dyad of two people, the next unit world of fellow men is probably a group of around five. Aristotle first suggested this number as where *society* begins.

At least five provides a community of interpretation, a constellation which can kindle flame in each other, a unit of creation and mutual growth, a reference group that tells us who we are and that we are significant. If five people believe in us and believe what we believe, then we can face a rough world.

Almost every great man in any field clusters around himself an inner circle—disciples who interpret to others what is being said and done and its importance. The trust and belief of these disciples in the pioneering originator frees him from gnawing anxiety that he is merely queer and on a snipe hunt. So his mind is free to create. Their conversation and questions sharpen up the focus, eliminate foolish errors. Their energies invent the ways that fundamental truth can enter into the bloodstream of events around them.

Such nuclear groups have brought off radically creative invention in social institutions, in scientific thought, in religious living, in philosophizing truth. We have underrated such groups in our excessive emphasis today upon each individual's making up his own mind, being totally original. Or in another mistaken style of life we collapse into slavish conformity to the fashion and trends of some mass herd movement which takes from us all responsibility for participating in creativity. Instead of a corporateness, we are a mob.

Clustering such a nuclear group is worth intending more

seriously than most of us do. We should be more determined to help organize and bring off such life world of fellow men. We cannot wait around for others to "start something" and bring us in.

Such a nuclear group does not have to have a genius or a star at its center. Perhaps in many situations, it is better that it not. But it must be a team of *fellow* men.

So we need to discover more about what makes a productive team.

Every productive team is matching itself against some significant opportunity or problem or crisis. The members explore, think, and talk together until their imaginations are stirred, and each has a fair idea of what can be born at this time and place.

Each must be able to enable the others to *become*. And so must learn how to address the creativity in the other rather than call up his frightened, defensive, angry self.

Increasingly we are becoming aware that at times everyone is in need of healing. At times everyone is so weakened in his self-respect that he is unusually fragile. So wounded by not being received by others that he moves out of the group's task to lick his wounds and nurse his resentment. There are dark moments and periods in every person's life when vision crumbles, and he experiences himself as unable to function as he usually does.

In the future, a good group member will have some skills as therapist. *And in all walks of life there will be increasing need for people able to handle conflict creatively.*

A WORLD LIFE WORLD

From this size group, life world leaps to all sizes. So let's make the greatest possible leap with Teilhard de Chardin.

The universe in which we are placed has been in millennia of travail toward the emergence of a world network of thinking men, deeply caring about each other, in honest communication with each other, each open to the lure of God to become more than he now is.

Your generation is privileged to live in this new human consciousness.

This goal of life world has been implicit in all that we have said so far. And without distracting from its total world dimension, we can realize this kind of life world in the heres and nows of all kinds of situations—whatever the number of people.

We can discover fellow men and bring off with them a *life* world.

This is quite different from just being a person well liked by everyone.

11

AN ORIGINATING FAMILY

Since for years resentful people have been criticizing the family, let's look at its possibilities.

POSSIBILITIES HIDDEN IN FAMILY

A family is an intimate attempt at a society of fellow men, i.e., of people who believe in each other.

Of whose faithfulness there is no end, distinguishes it from most other groups. You care about each other throughout life. Not just while on a brief journey together as in most friendships in this very mobile world. Home is the place you can go even if all the other doors are shut. What makes it home and family is creative fidelity which may be defined as continuing delight in each other's growth.

Family is generativity. A unit of personality-making. An institute of human development.

Here the great words and meaningful experiences of our civilization first come to us. Here we enter culture. We are all only variations of our family's style of life. In the family are the origins of conscience, our trust in others, our self as initiating center. Always, the family is a prime determiner of how we feel about ourselves.

The family is an especially realistic place for our growth. We can get constant report on how we affect other people—if we want to. We can discover what we do and feel under pressure. We can't just walk off if we get in conflict. In the family we have to live it through—for the same people are there next day.

The family is about the only place where different ages of people live with each other. So life's continuities are built and the generations of man personally influence each other. All ages profit. There could be no worse world for adults than one without young people or children, nothing worse for young people than a world only of teen-agers—with no adults or children around. For very few adolescents want to remain permanently as teen-agers. They want to find entrance into the adult world. So they want a father and a mother who are no longer father-mother of the child they once were, but of themselves—now-becoming-adults. They need parents who are not permanently frozen at the place they entered adult life years ago, but are in the thick of things *now*.

It is better, even if difficult, to have available the viewpoints and desires of more than one age group in any civilization. For more range and novelty feed into the culture. And the necessity of finding some threads to weave it all together is upon everyone.

Finally the family is a manageable unit of culture and relationship. It is a size of society not beyond our powers to co-create and co-manage.

All these possibilities are the very nature of a family. Since we all realize them imperfectly, there is no family where further growth in them is impossible.

WHY TREAT THESE POSSIBILITIES ABSURDLY?

If these are its possibilities, why do some families do so poorly?

Partly because of the fanciful expectation that once people are married, they just "naturally" live happily ever after. That anybody—the most careless, irresponsible, immature—can make a marriage work. All that is needed is two people infatuated, dependent on each other. Love isn't anything that involves the repeated investment of the best of yourself.

Marriage and raising children is the last area of life in our civilization which we trust to amateurs who have no understanding of what they are doing and no tested method.

The worst absurdity which our society cultivates about the foundations of family, however, is a mistrust of love. Nourished by entertainment and nightclub celebrities, by novelists, playwrights, and by divorce statistics, love-starved people become uneasy when a relationship begins to deepen. For they know how to handle only love's trivialized forms. So they pretend that marriage and family living and children aren't really importantly life. Life is elsewhere. Marriage and family is certainly no life world—so they declare. At best it can be expected—and ought—to disintegrate after a few years. "Who wants to be so old-fashioned as to live in troth to someone?"—so this viewpoint suggests.

Yet people continue to "vote" overwhelmingly for marriage and for "having" a family (not the same as *being* a family). Even the divorced quickly rush back into marriage.

As for you—you want it to be something whose meaning and possibilities you understand. You intend a spirited family. You want to know, "When it *is* marriage and family, what is it?" So that you and yours don't let it wither on the vine because of absurdities and stupidities.

WHAT MAKES IT A FAMILY?

What enables these possibilities of marriage, family, home? Let's concentrate on five things—I-Thou, creative fidelity, communication, healthy sex, and a family tradition. A handful of family.

I-THOU

The family is one place where we can be free to be aware of each other as persons.

We do not need to be all the time demanding production and achievement from each other. Or to be a nagging, biting conscience for the other.

We can take time to treat each other as *subjects*. We can meet each other head-on as unique way of feeling and seeing things. And be really interested in how each other sees and feels significantly. We can experience other members of our family as power struggling to bring off the project of their own lives, as sufferers of dark moments and need for healing and atoning. For we encounter them when they are a defensive shut-up-ness as well as when they are permeable and open. We can have sense enough to keep areas of freedom and playfulness in the home—openings where each can actualize himself without immediately having someone else try to take it over and fill it with himself.

On the occasions that "I's" and "Thous" exist in a family, we live as depth, openness, originating aliveness.

CREATIVE FIDELITY

A family is people who genuinely care about each other—even in conflict and battle. They care about each other and what each does and is.

If they didn't care, there would be no conflicts or struggle. They would be indifferent to each other, ignore each other, wear poker faces and never feel passionately about what is happening. What a world that would be. Anything would go—each person would try to have the world as *he* wanted it, on his terms, and immediately. He would be *non*-personal.

An exciting new picture of family is emerging with the realization that each era of the life of a person has its distinctive crises and opportunities in the development of that person as fully human. Each member of a family is in the midst of some new breaking out. It is going on simultaneously! Everyone is trying to get his becoming done at the same time everybody else is doing his. An adolescent son has to establish that he can make good decisions *on his own,* at about the time father is wondering whether his one life on earth will ever mean anything. His mother is in the same destiny struggle. Further, she has to face the fact that she is no longer an adolescent beauty queen. Son, father, mother are all uncertain and

93

jittery; each covers up with surface imperviousness. All three need talk in which they can just kick things around without somebody jumping all over them and trying to take over their lives. They all need help rather than further hindrances to their growing.

Intelligent fidelity to the other's growth (and not just to his creature comforts) makes one truly a parent, and truly son or daughter.

Biological parenthood is not enough. It is merely the beginning. *Human* parenthood is fidelity to the *growth of their children as persons*. And since we now see that fathers and mothers have growing to do, we also see that sons and daughters have the special privilege of being good friends of their parents' growth.

But the nucleus out of which any family grows is the creative fidelity of husband and wife to each other. If this center holds, no enemies can destroy the family or the people in it.

The dyad of husband and wife must take precedence over any other relationship. Else the family breaks up into jealous units. The children have no model of fidelity and I-Thou to interiorize as a style of personal relations. Each child's own personality has at its heart two warring factions —love and identification with father, love and identification with mother. Unless *actually* in real life mother and father are together, the child has problems putting these two lives together inside himself. And in the meantime, he gets caught in their battle, either having to choose sides or play them one against the other in the service of his own immature desires.

Creative fidelity to each other's growth and to co-creation together is the essence of being a husband to someone, and a wife to someone.

COMMUNICATION

Much communication—particularly in a family—is non-verbal. All the time, everything we do has its language. People may not talk much—but their acts, their bodies, their gestures (the lift of an eyebrow, the tenseness of a face) communicate. The *tone* of voice in which a person talks is expressing how he feels about himself, about the person he is talking to, and his state of conviction about what he is saying.

Children learn very early to listen to the *tone* of father's and mother's voices, rather than to the words they are using. This ability to catch the feeling out of which people are talking is what makes a good listener and a good developer of conversation. For inside and within the feeling there is more than the person has yet said, and it is feeling which is moving the speaker. All husbands, wives, parents should have further training in this skill.

Every family establishes a pattern and style of communication which largely determines the worthwhileness of its being together. Family policy may be to close off communication about anything important or about differences and conflict. Father or mother may set a pattern of clamming up or breaking out in violent anger—just when there is greatest need for getting things out in the open and dealing with them.

95

The crucial quality of any communication is its honesty.

Do a mother's sweetly modulated tones harmonize with what she is actually doing to the child? If not, she is pernicious. For she is giving two conflicting signals and the child gets horribly confused and messed up. Many college-educated mothers have learned this kind of communication as a way of life. They have become skilled in duplicity and phoniness in many areas of life. And so have fathers and husbands. So who knows what is real in the other? Finally, *who knows what is real?*

Young people put a real strain on the communication of a family which may take some years to work through. They themselves are in a communication bind. On one hand they have to come to terms with their own peer culture, and a part of it is always brutal in its rejection of people who are different. On the other hand they also need to stay in relationship with their parents and very much need some trustworthy adult with whom to think things through. How does a young person bring off new life and gain courage to make his own decisions, but remain in communication with the family out of which he is springing? A certain reserve and silence and difference is necessary to protect his fragile newness.

Many young people declare a war between generations. Everybody born before a certain date is hopelessly stupid and should be killed off (psychologically in the teenager's mind, if not actually in the world).

It is natural for every teen-ager to be like the young duck, commemorated in a Japanese haiku:

The young wild duck
Looks as if it was saying:
"I've been down to the bottom and
seen everything."

After the first dive into life, he was sure he knew all there was to be known about the lake.

Each new generation does represent possibility of a new destiny and so must understand the genius of its new movement. It will have to learn to handle a world the parents' generation cannot. But *presently* some adults are already living toward desirable future, and it is important to establish connections with them. For it is not so much *when* he was born, but sensitivity to desirable future, that makes one important to know.

Present-day adults—compared with the world they have to *handle*—are stupid. But who *is* allwise?

In any case, an adolescent ought to have a better authority on basic issues of life than a celebrity in the entertainment world or a disc jockey. For the stakes in life are more than entertainment. Yet many teen-agers are saturated with the gods and goddesses of mass entertainment. Who is he to really listen to?

Perhaps if we know of this communication bind in a family with young people—and of the necessity of its tensions—we can live through it better.

It is important in a family to treat each other as making the good try and take time to listen, even if the parent has to make the final decision on some issues and the adolescent on others.

•

97

HEALTHY SEX

Having established some understanding of I-Thou, creative fidelity, and communication, we can comprehend what healthy sex is.

Sex relations of husband and wife can be the most productive, pleasurable, meaningful of any sex relations. For then sex is placed in totalness and depth of existence, rather than experienced as a burning fragment of entertainment. Between husband and wife, sexual intercourse can be an act and a symbol of a life of co-creation and glad giving without reservation. Marriage is the one place where they can learn that mating is for the purpose of co-creation, not just tension release.

Sex is located in the context of creation. Creation refers to offspring, the participating by two people in the plot and play of life on this earth as it comes through them. Creation also refers to the realization of personal existence in themselves which comes through healthy sex.

The quality of sexual intercourse depends primarily upon the meaningfulness of life for the two persons involved. For sex is the physical interfused with culture (meanings of life).

Sex is personal relationship—relational event and interpersonal art. Healthy sexual experience is an endeavor to break through the walls of flesh to direct union of the all of one's self with the all of the other person. The endeavor of two individual centers of awareness, held apart by individual experience and physical structures of the body, to come into direct and unimpeded union with each other. The warm embrace, the vigorous kiss, the deep penetration are all evidences of the intensity of this desire to achieve union with the inner core of the other person.

And so it is intensely *enjoyable* to the degree that it is uniting two authentic persons. For then sex is truly realizing its impulse.

The human sex act is an expression of trust. Between the two people there already exists a relationship of creative fidelity, communication, continuity. For the inherent nature of sexual intercourse is giving the all of one's self without reservation. And (unless we are incredibly naïve) we can do this only with someone who knows us as we really are and is willing to be known as he really is. And regards us as worthy of devotion in ways other than just this moment. And we regard ourselves and them as such kind of person.

Mature sex is an expressive act, not a necessary or compulsive one. An offering to each other of our feeling life and our possibilities for future action. And so is *part of* the fusing of two personal histories. Since man is constituted by *time*, sex must be part of a story of life —that includes both partners.

Healthy sex is not divorced from the rest of life's activities. The more we bring into it, the more intense the experience. So sex is consummation and celebration of total life together. And of common life story. It is a most vivid "natural" sacrament. And therefore when profaned, turns our life into absurdity and boring triviality.

All this is what we *really* mean by "sex." The word is used to cover a number of things which are anti-sex. Such as Kinsey's concept of "sex outlets" (a purely biological classification) or the use of sex to prove something ("I really am a *male*—or female"), or as an act of successful aggression and domination, or of frightened submission in order to be admitted to an ingroup, or to achieve status, or "to make love." All these are quite far from the real article. They pretend to be sex, but rightfully should be called "anti-sex."

Anti-sex habits and mediocre concepts of sexual intercourse make it quite difficult to experience joyful marriage. It would seem right to move toward the real article in marriage, becoming now the kind of person able to bring off full partnership and mutuality.

Healthy sex is an act of *persons*. Persons interfused with culture. Persons growing out of I-Thou, creative fidelity, communication, and meanings.

STARTING A FAMILY TRADITION: THIS FAMILY'S CULTURE

We are all suffering today because adults have been lacking in values, convictions, culture. And in the courage to make manifest in their community and effective in their homes those which they have.

You don't have to live that way.

Many husbands and wives have never had a lengthy serious conversation about their values and convictions —except perhaps in angry agreement that their children ought to obey better and do better in school. They wouldn't know how to go about having such a discussion. Few have understood very clearly what makes a family.

Nor clearly seen that they are managers of an "ours-to-make" culture and tradition.

A home is not just a nice car, or a house nicely furnished, or available food and money. It is not simply a place to entertain the husband's business customers. All that is merely a nice smooth sleekness.

A home is a *culture*. Where one meets people of convictions—who are also able to talk and reason about them. A home is a society. And there is no society without some established rights and wrongs, some basic conscience to which every member is responsible. A home is a place where the whole family meets interesting people who have been places and done things. A home is a cluster of people each in contact with the issues of the larger society.

A family is a unit of civilization. The father and mother must be its chief originators and architects. But to keep it alive, all members must take part in making a living tradition.

For example, certain words take on special meaning for *this* family group. Certain ways of celebrating what has happened distinguish it from other families. Over a period of time family lore develops, the house becomes suffused with human experiences and memories. The family begins to understand what civilization is all about. And has a tradition that its members serve civilization.

Inescapably a family is a certain quality of life. A culture. Which all the time it is deciding for—usually without knowing that it is. Or ever talking together about what quality and culture they intend, or are having. The family, as culture, is often totally unpremeditated, unmeant. The

101

product of happenstance and the pressures of outside forces anxious to sell and use the family's members for its own purposes. Why be this stupid?

Pulse a family tradition into existence that has style. Originate.

12

A JOB THAT BECOMES LIFE WORLD

A job is access into a world. It opens you into reality other than yourself. But unless that reality becomes a meaningful world, your job is drudgery rather than work.

Your world of work must have the qualities of life world. Else you become a nothingness. Often become demonic.

"I INHABIT IT"

The first quality of a life world is "I inhabit it. This is habitat for me."

This does not mean that here is all your life. That there is no other place where you may be found. But it does mean—

> "I am *here*. *I am* here.
> Something importantly myself is in it.
> As feeling, thinking, relating to others,
> projecting enterprises of my one life on earth,
> I *live* in this."

The prefix "in" of "inhabit" does not mean "*contained* in," but "*participating* in." It is most unsatisfying and unproductive to be *contained in* a job. "Participating in" means "I saturate the available world with the quality and intentions of my life. I invest in this world my motives, values, imagination, hopes—as well as my technical know-how. I make offering of these, so it really becomes a place where life is celebrated."

. It is, of course, easier to do this in the service industries and in the professions than in many assembly-line jobs. But unless you do the best you can to work on a job in this participating, putting-your-integrity-into-it way, then you are alienated man—estranged from the working of your body, from the corporation you are part of, and from your inner-personal core.

And only you can make of your job life world.

The firm (in particular the administrators and the president) does help or hinder. So do fellow employees and the prevailing work climate. Life world is always a "we-world," i.e., a co-creation. Every firm or institution for which we work gives a necessary particular context to our lives, so that we get defined, take on content, form, muscle. We become *something*, rather than vague diffuseness. We acquire a *style* of life. To belong to any institution offers us a purpose, plan, method by which our lives escape total meaninglessness, planlessness, anomie.

But finally the person determines and decides whether he is engaged in drudgery or work. It is—or is not—a staging area of his life. He has selected out, helped organize, helped determine the quality of this world. Other people are present and part of it, but here are moments of aliveness for him.

INHABITED BY OTHER PERSONS

Other people also have to *be there* for a job to become a meaningful world. A totally impersonal or anti-personal work situation becomes no longer a place to work or a place of *work*.

"Inhabited by persons" does not mean social gadgetry. Coffee breaks, for instance, may become infectious sources of nonhuman and anti-personal relationships. If people are personal, it comes out where they meaningfully and normally encounter each other. The man who grunts instead of saying "good morning" may be—when the chips are down—more fully personal then the one who speaks.

If—as we have said in an earlier section—*a person* is a life that deeply cares, that lives toward some horizon in decisiveness and integrity, *with* fellow human beings, then we know what we mean when we say that a work life world is inhabited by persons.

The workers are very imperfect persons, of course. But there is a minimal mutuality and trust that the others will come through. Ways of getting gripes out of your system and getting something done about them do get established. Some people at least adopt the policy, "Keep being personal yourself; why join the blokes?"

If—in order for it to cease being impersonal—the whole vast universe has to come to us in the form of a person, so does every institution or organization for which we work.

Somebody—for us—has to symbolize in his own person what the organization is about, what standards and quality of work we expect of ourselves, what climate of personal relationships is possible. "The boss" is the official candidate for this function. The president of the company better be this sort of person, or the future is bleak. Often a fellow employee is this for us. We always need to find both kinds of symbol people—fellow workers and people who sit at the crossroads of power.

And we have to find a guarantor.

A guarantor is one of the kinds of persons we have just considered, who notices us, sometimes talks to us as man to man, gives us an important job to do with freedom to carry it out, in confidence that we can. And so altogether gives us the feeling that—being what we are and can become—we have a future here.

A little world inhabited by persons, then, is one thing that makes work a life world. People's perceptions of each other and the interpersonal are a large part of the reality of any work situation. And perhaps an even larger part of its satisfyingness.

But unless *you* dwell *in* this interpersonal world—and *in* the work enterprise which the organization exists to bring off—it cannot be a world of persons. It is no *life world* for you.

If you are to be at home in your job, there is a third necessity. You must see it as an opening in which you can actualize your one life on earth—meaningfully.

AN OPENING FOR YOURSELF AS PROJECT OF A LIFE ON EARTH

Whether consciously or not, we are always organizing a staging area for our life. With more or less of ourselves involved. We are so built that restlessly we keep searching for *an opening into significance*.

A job is work rather than drudgery to the degree you believe in the product. And therefore that your life has some significance. That you are not pouring it down a rat hole or merely making your money there.

It is at this point that many people today lose respect for themselves because they question what their lives are going into. For so much of industry and research is aimed at producing ways of destroying human beings. "Is my life fulfilled by enabling men to destroy life?"

A job is work only if we feel that it gives us a chance to actualize *meaningful* world. In today's world we have to take initiative about selecting and organizing the "place where" our realization can take place.

Work is a making and remaking of the world—not just transporting a pile of bricks from one place to another. There is room in *work* to enterprise a conquest over chaos and resistant material, and to project yourself ahead of what now is. In drudgery there is no such room.

Which finally means that the purposes of the organization for which you work and the goals of your life have to be going in the same direction. The institution ought to have a history which you know. It ought to have a head (perhaps yourself!) capable of interpreting what human need it is matching itself against and how and where the crucial issues now are. Else you are not engaged in *work*.

Every business firm must make profits in order to keep improving the quality of its services and its product. But profit just for the sake of profit is a dismal goal for a man's life on earth. Every business is not only responsible for its specific target of human need and fulfillment but for thinking how a viable social-economic order can be made possible over the world. An industry is responsible for making widely available to the mass market the necessities of life at the lowest possible cost consistent with quality. So that the masses may become *elite*. The same responsibility lies upon educational and cultural institutions.

WORK AS IF MEMBER OF A PROFESSION

In the future, no matter what our job—be it mother, teacher, worker, manager, doctor—we all will have to live *as if* we were members of a great professional group. It is the professions which make possible man beyond the subsistence level. They are the middle class without which civilization is impossible. They are the self-disciplined groups upon which progress depends.

What is it to live as a member of a great profession?

It is to experience one's self as part of a world community of concerned people which matches itself against some great human need. Carrying on for all mankind frontier exploration in that specific enterprise.

To participate in a profession is to have a philosophy of civilization and a definition of what it means to be a person. And to refuse to violate that vision or desecrate human dignity. It is to be "a teacher who put out extra effort to cause each student to realize his potential."

It is to have fundamental truth. Saving, enabling truth, whose transmission and leaps forward are the striving of our lives.

It is to have standards of quality functioning to which

we hold ourselves and others. Less than this we will not tolerate nor keep still about.

It is to be in communication with those all over the world who are so engaged. Withholding nothing which will set forward the fundamentals of our common fate and enterprise.

The next step in civilization is for all work to become greatly a profession.

You don't have to be a member of the so-called "great professions" to live this way or to have this quality life world.

On to the place where you *work!*

13

LEISURE TIME WORLD

Leisure time is no longer what a person does to rest up from work. To release him from the tensions built up from work and send him back in the morning able to endure another day.

Once people thought that leisure time had no value in and of itself. That one should be ashamed of it. Its value was only relative to a person's work. But to a modern mind, leisure time has its own values. It too is a situation where a person experiences fulfillment of himself as person or becomes a nothingness.

Leisure time has become a "world." Definitely life, and not a footnote to life.

AUTHENTIC LEISURE TIME

Leisure time is life space that a person freely chooses. Activities where he experiences himself spontaneously functioning. Overflowing. There are no crippling worries and anxieties, no persons ordering him around and saying "no." Chronological time (the determinism of the clock) loses its tyranny and for the moment is no more. Meaningful time takes over. The person becomes utterly absorbed, forgetful of the slings and arrows of outrageous fortune.

For the moment he is transcendence. In charge of potential, rather than being demanded of.

Fulfillment rather than release from tensions; *creation* rather than recreation; self-propelled *spontaneity* rather than being led around by the nose; playful *expressiveness* rather than performing a grim duty; the *culturing* of man —all these are in the new thinking about leisure time and leisure world.

CONDITIONS BRINGING ABOUT THE NEW VIEW

How did we get here?

Partly because we no longer have to work from sunrise to sunset just to get enough to eat. We no longer have to work all week. We have time for culture.

Partly because we think that it is not right for a person's job to become a god demanding the sacrifice of all his mind, to be the sole shaper of his personality, to suck out of him his last ounce of energy. Even a Moloch requiring the sacrifice of his children.

Partly because all over the world people are rising up and demanding that they be treated as persons. Asserting with everything they are that they are not machines or peasants but human beings. And mean to be so. They believe they have a right to function *as person*.

It is not enough to feed, house, clothe, and work a *man*. He requires time and opportunity for culturing.

New views about leisure time have come also because there is enough of it that we begin to see we can do something with it, that it is *a world*. And it's becoming evident that many of the leisure time life worlds people are creating are sickness and evasion of life.

HOW TO CHOOSE AND ORGANIZE A LEISURE TIME WORLD

If leisure time is part of your making of yourself, if it is opportunity to spot fresh openings in which your energies can expand and enjoy functioning, you have a lot of interesting choices ahead of you. You will progressively select out a leisure world which is *your* habitat. You can't just let other people organize and program it for you, but must follow your sense of where and what life is for you.

Leisure time world will be tailored by and for each unique person.

You can't live all the possibilities now offered by leisure world, but you can do better than the narrow confines and ruts many around you fall into. You were meant to *be* —and generously. To have some sense that over a period of time you are actualizing the full orb of being person as you want to be. And further, not settle into everything at a superficial level, for satisfaction requires a certain amount of competence. In some things you ought to be at least an amateur professional.

What might make up a list of leisure world possibilities?

Currently, for some people, the long weekend is the time for orgy and killing off awareness—particularly self-awareness. But that soon goes into bankruptcy, since its sole aim is tension release and escape from—rather than healing—what's wrong with us and the world. It assumes that irresponsibility will set everything right. But raising hell is not a very significant measure of being a man.

Another nomination would be amusement and entertainment. Amusement and entertainment we all need. To see a good play, hear a funny comedian, flavor the tonal nuances and intersubjectivity of a good combo, have the luck to see an exceptional movie—these are good. But alone, they are very partial and inadequate use of free time. And must never become the sole source of interpretation of the meaning of life or of the goals of life. Strange as it may seem to the amusement-intoxicated, the entertainment world is not the *whole,* nor the *center,* of *civilization.*

Conversation with people we like to be around—and who have sense enough to find something fresh to talk about or at least some new angles—is the most common universal leisure time activity. And something all of us would like to develop.

As for humor, let it flash whenever it can. For humor is ourselves leaping out of our skins, poking fun at ourselves and at pretentiousness wherever it is, getting a distance and perspective on our troubles, seeing the absurdities of our current events and communities. When it is not merely misguided aggression, humor is playfulness at its best.

In the years ahead, we will increasingly hunger to realize beauty. The beauty of mountain and lake and trees. The beauty of a house that expresses simply and well the values of the family living there. Clothes which do likewise. Beauty in fragments of poetry—such as haiku. Beauty of line, color, composition in pictures. Beauty in

113

music and song. Beauty in the body's doing well what it is trying to do. Beauty of spirit.

Good taste will increasingly characterize our leisure world.

We can also have more of ourselves in our leisure world. Leisure world can be more an *expression of ourselves* than just whiling away time. Leisure world is creative world—if we do not allow ourselves to be dragged into being merely consumers.

We already have too many people living secondhand out of the meanings other people suggest. Who do not nurture their own lived moments into something expressive of their own depth.

In the world of the future, we need to be persons who will let some beauty hidden in life flow into words, imagery, music. And take significant shape. By such activity we transmute the world and ourselves into meaning. Without it, it is as if we never lived.

For man *is* a *cultured* creature. We should be about creating *man*. And today he needs more, not less, meanings. We have enough superficial meanings. We need some of depth.

One good use of leisure time then is to create culture —symbols expressive of our glimpse into life, meanings which we discover we are living by.

The startling and massive new development in leisure time is electronic communications—radio, TV, movies. Today's people must learn how to use radio and TV as a means of expanding awareness of the world and the possibilities of life, without becoming enslaved by it and substituting it for firsthand experience. There is real danger that more leisure time will merely result in more sitting, more nothingness filled with sound and fury and aloneness.

But our goal relative to "blip" communications is not merely defensive—though it has to be that. Electronic communication is the shaper of a new mode of human consciousness for everybody. Such a leap that happens once in millennia. We should help it become that—both in its programming and in our personal use of TV.

Whatever happens, TV, radio, recordings will fill much of the leisure time we have right in our own room.

To rescue us from passivity and from a deathly curling back in on ourselves, a leisure world should include fighting as a volunteer in some good cause where we are in new contact with the courage (and plain cussedness) of people, involved in a new common fate with others toward a horizon we are not paid to march toward.

Such a natural and "at hand" cause as being friends and guarantors to the children of our community would do wonders to us. But we should also have a cause which unites us with people radically different from ourselves.

The nature of free time (saying "yes" to new openings) also means times of letting go and letting what will, well up in our feelings and minds. Can you listen to great music *without* this happening? Yes, if you keep talking all the time and use it merely for noise to fill your empty heart! Can you stand being alone and quiet—outdoors or in—and let more of yourself well up in your mind? Or ponder on what something really is? Or reading a book, lay it down and let your thoughts soar? Then you have the beginnings of tuning in to life via yourself. Leisure time is for the discovery of one's depths, rather than for becoming more and more dependent upon a constant stream of stimuli coming from outside.

Religious celebration in a communal group is also to be explored. The celebration together of a people who have gone through battles together, who have participated in history-making, who are setting out through time toward a destiny, who trust each other, is one of the rare privileges granted man. Would that more church services were such religious celebration.

Each year—or at least every three or four years—we ought to open up some new area of exploration—Chinese civilization, existential psychology, communications, photography, badminton, to mention but illustrations. And don't just "take up" photography. Go into what the strikingly original photographers were trying to do *until you understand how it is to exist as a person—as they understood it.* For it is at this level that life is revealed to you. You are then not just a technician.

If man does live in culture and meanings, rather than in sensations, then this conception of leisure world makes sense. Find the openings for you. And there you will find happiness, rather than trying to hunt it up.

14

THE PUBLIC OPINION
YOU HELP FORM

Another most important staging area of your life is the public opinion *in* which you live. Here, as elsewhere among these chapters, "in" does not mean "contained in," but "participating in."

YOU DO LIVE IN PUBLIC OPINION

You live as person only because you are constantly breathing an atmosphere of public opinion.

Public opinion is a little universe which man creates within the vast physical universe. Without public opinion, people couldn't be *together,* couldn't get anything done which required common effort. Society, a community—and your mind—is created and held together by public opinion.

Encountering public opinion and living *in* it keeps your mind alive. And gives you a chance to live out of meanings rather than brute event. Public opinion is an expression of a people's *culture*—meanings and views commonly understood and held, out of which all sorts of ideas and proposals come.

No wonder it can be so tyrannical as well as life-giving. No wonder we easily fall into pressurized conformity so that our flight through life will be comfortable.

HOW IS IT TO LIVE IN PUBLIC OPINION?

How does it feel to live *in* public opinion? Much of the time, it feels awfully good. We know what we can do and what we can get people to rally for. We feel confirmed and affirmed. We are right kind of folk and of sound judgment. We have companions on our journey of life. We understand our world and the goals of life in about the same way; we interpret news and events in about the same way. And we all know that this is so. So we trust each other.

No one can live very long without such participation in the public opinion of a society of at least five people. Anyone who intends to be self-propelling life, rather than merely taking it on the chin, will be active in organizing such a miminal world of public opinion for himself where he can really live. Sometimes the five cluster around two. Five is about the workable size where everybody can talk, differences can·be threshed out, a creative idea can really roll instead of being stultified or smothered before it even has a chance to breathe.

But public opinion is often quaggy marsh seeping in all directions. Living *in* public opinion is very fear-producing. Nobody knows where to stand, for he doesn't know where solid ground is Both adults and young people are lost in a swamp. Out of the dark, in all directions voices call, "This is the way to life."

Then too, we often find ourselves where public opinion is very stupid and determined to cut down excellence and make life mediocre. This crowd mind is cruel—happily destroying those who stand out with reasoned conviction. And the more guilty, fearful, and uncertain people are, the more viciously they attack anyone who tries to embody justice and intelligence. Today many people experience this kind of public opinion and must learn how to deal with it.

Public opinion is often terrorism. It does not feel good at all to live in it.

But whatever its quality, public opinion sets much of the *feeling tone* of your life as well as its direction. And one's mode of participating in public opinion forms him to be either a crawling worm or a person walking through life with a spine.

CREATE, FORM; DON'T JUST ENDURE PUBLIC OPINION

One goal of life then is to help *create* public opinion rather than just float on it; to *form* it, rather than just endure it. To build culture, rather than to moan about how horrible it is where we are.

People who are making the good try in life must live an *expressive* life. Put their fumbling ideas into words and get them out into the marketplace of ideas, i.e., their own group, their community, their profession, the public mind. Too often the decent, thoughtful people keep silent and let public opinion be formed by the dolts and loudmouthed smear artists. And today we have these in every community.

Even while in school, a person's basic pattern of participating in public opinion is laid down.

Some "students" in a classroom sit there passively, requiring of the teacher that they be aroused and educated. They haven't the faintest thought that they are responsible for whether the class chases and develops an idea. They

119

keep muttering under their breath but never risk trying to hold their own with teacher or fellow students. Because deep down they feel inferior, they pretend to a wisdom too precious to expose to other people. They permanently learn irresponsibility in a common enterprise of public opinion.

There are also those who prattle. Verbally very facile, they can trivialize anything. Once in their family tree, there was someone whose opinion people wanted to hear!

What is a teacher to do? Talk personally with those who are trying to create views and develop ideas, instead of spending so much time, as he now does, with the excuse-givers? Perhaps help a student discover that he does have a good idea?

Whatever is expected of a teacher, it is each student's responsibility and privilege *as human* to take his share in creating ideas and a climate of co-creation.

Let us celebrate the thinking, feeling, symbolizing, communicating person. The person skilled in the great conversation.

THE GREAT CONVERSATION AS THE CENTRAL TOOL

Down through the centuries vivid men have carried on the great conversation. They have talked about the issues of life, with a play of mind upon mind where each builds out of what the other has stirred in him. Minds stab each other out of sleepy laziness, and sloppy thinking is surgically treated. They have done this in evening meals together. Cicero prided himself that he and his Roman friends met for such talk, whereas the Greeks met to drink. The Hebrew Chaburah celebrated a religious meal together and then talked for the evening. In early America men gathered around the stove in the store or in the public square to talk over news, experiences, yarns, life philosophy. And such great conversation has been their meat and drink.

You can make possible for yourself such meaningful conversation. Train yourself in its art, keep acquiring enough ideas for it to be exciting. Help form a group of kindred minds with which to communicate and co-create. And finally, communicate to a larger public.

To function well in such a group, the necessary skills and habits must be acquired. *One necessary skill is to receive another's feeling and ideas in such a way that it grows and develops.*

Further, you must know how to keep the conversation going until the *significant symbol* emerges. This takes time. *Significant symbol* means a key policy, idea, event, or person that everybody involved understands in about the same way, and it calls forth in everybody about the same attitude. And everybody finally knows that this condition exists. It is called "significant"—because now a *society* exists, where before there were only separate individuals. Now they can work together and trust each other. Every business firm, school, church, country is held together and moved by significant symbol.

AN AGENT OF MEANING

To be an agent enabling meanings to develop in other people is a significant part of your life. For to live out of meanings, rather than in the pushes and pulls of vegetative and biological life, distinguishes life at the *human* level from all other life. You are helping them to become human.

And we live in a time when there is need of sharp thinking on what life is all about and what meanings it can have. The market is flooded by many cheap substitutes for the real article.

To work on significant meanings of life, to put them into beautiful embodiment in your living, in memorable words and conversation, in music, poems, paintings that express the meaning that you see and feel, is really much of what life is about. To symbolize faint stirrings and fleeting glimpses of new life is important—otherwise they are lost forever. And only if they are symbolized can you communicate them to others.

You owe this ministry to your fellow man.

A CELEBRATION OF COMMUNICATION

Thus you will be a very fundamental process of life —communication.

If today we were writing another set of Ten Commandments, one about communication would be very near the top. This "commandment" would say that to choose life, you have to choose communication. And *honesty* of communication is a touchstone of one's integrity.

It would say that communication is a two-way circuit —not a monologue. That it consists both of expressing and of receiving. And it would make clear that communication is communion and co-creation, an offering of ourselves to God and man. And so participates in Mystery.

15

MAKE HISTORY

Because your life occurs in some stream of history-making, it is possible for you to become a person.

YOU FORM OUT OF A PEOPLE

You were born into a world of persons already highly organized. A world which has been going on for a long time before you ever arrived and will be here after you have gone. Neither the world nor wisdom begins with you.

THE GREAT WORDS OF CIVILIZATION

You were born into a particular world of persons. From hearing these persons talk as they went about life, you acquired a language.

After due time, their *spoken* words became your *speaking* words—the language you felt, thought, decided, communicated with. These words enabled you to symbolize your experience, present it to yourself and to others. If it had been required of you to invent a language of your own, your life would have been over before you hardly got started on the task. And few people would understand the grunts you could utter, for your "words" would be empty of the experiencing of many centuries of people.

To organize a lighted-up life world for yourself, you must immerse yourself in the great words of civilization until *you* live *in* them and they come alive in your experiences.

This is a vast task—for the reality isn't the words themselves.

Somehow you have to get back to the experiences,· encounter for yourself the realities which the words symbolize, simultaneous with your use of the word.

YOUR PEOPLE'S PARADIGM EXPERIENCES

The words are only *symbols* of great lived moments. Only symbols of great insights into life. They are only *ways of representing* these lived moments and felt significances to yourself. If you have never confronted or experienced anything that word is referring to, then it is noise, paper chicken tracks, no-sense to you.

So you have to live vigorously. The great words cannot function for you until you yourself have lived the paradigm experiences of our civilization. What is a paradigm?

Every civilization, every "people" (as well as every person) is a cluster of recurring experiences.

They recur because the society wants them to happen again. Why? In these experiences the meaning of life breaks through. The meaning of this society's history becomes manifest. Incarnated. The society comes alive.

Freedom, for example, is one of the great paradigms. It is in the American heritage, in the Judeo-Christian heritage. But we keep on struggling only because we have some taste of freedom and some expectancy toward it.

The scientific method of inventing new things is a paradigm of contemporary civilization all over the world.

Such core experiences hold together both the person and the civilization. They provide dependable, expected ways of getting the good life. They give dynamic. They set imagination in motion. They flavor and govern many other experiences of life.

So possess the paradigms of your people as well as the great words and imagery of your civilization.

ITS GREAT PERSONALIZATIONS AND STORY

To be understood and to take up residence in you, the great civilizing experiences and words have to come to you in the form of fascinating, powerful persons. So that you wish to be like them, share in their power. You see what *a person* really can be, how a person of dimensions functions. Through identification with them, something of *their person* takes up residence in you and you are nevermore the same.

So immerse yourself in biographies, encounter people who are these paradigms—freedom, justice, covenant, truth-seeking, pioneering, faith, meaningful suffering.

Hear and read and feel enough history that you can enter it from the inside, *stand in* it, relive it somewhat as it was experienced and interpreted by those involved in it. Until, while seeing its mistakes and dead ends, you so identify with it that you can function as a part of its present becoming. Dialogue with it, connect the struggle

125

of our times with it until some sequence of future-past-present stirs your imagination and calls up limitless energy in you.

Thus you can take part meaningfully in history. And with some understanding. Not as a dumb ox before the slaughterers. Or as a virulent edition of past stupidities and brutalities. For you will have found an encompassing horizon for the journey of your life. To some degree you will be able to interpret history-as-it-happens. Which is the ability mankind now has to acquire somehow.

Since man is that creature who lives in a meaningful world rather than in bare event and mere energy exchange, since he lives as meaningful time in chronological time, maybe this is your most important life world. Particularly if you place within it other forms of life world.

MAKE HISTORY: DON'T JUST ENDURE IT

Each generation must do history-making.

To try to stand outside man's present becoming would be to become a nothingness.

To take part in the contemporary struggles of your fellow man is a given of your life. So insert your life into some stream of present history-making and cause something better to happen.

The possibilities of your life are set in a particular length of history-making. You live in the second half of the twentieth century, and so have quite different realities to shape life in than any other era of the long, long journey of man.

A new mode of worldwide human consciousness is

emerging. Via television and other electronic media we are all now living *"in the same village."* Filled with all kinds of tribal tom-toms, conflicts breaking out on every street, everybody insisting he is meant to be a person. But a *world culture* is being formed—particularly among the young people of the world. You can participate importantly in such history-making. In the United States we have new opportunity in the ancient struggle to establish liberty and justice for all. And we must live the future that is now being formed in our midst, not rest dangerously in the past. We must move forward into a new freedom and power for the Negro and for the white man in our country. We are in process of trying to invent a viable economic and business order—for *the world*.

And, being well on our way to conquering the world of nature, we have human nature to explore and develop. We can turn our energies into new understandings of the depths of personal and interpersonal life. And through the art and religions, we can culture the meanings by which we as fellow citizens can keep becoming more fully human. New modes of communication are at our finger tips. The possibilities of history-making are now limitless. And catastrophic.

Each of us now has to live a prophet's life.

A prophet is a man who feels deeply what is going on in his moment of history. He cares about what is happening to people. For him, injustice is a catastrophe to the world—the destruction of what constitutes a *human* order. The violation of the human dignity of any child, of its chance to become as fully a person as is possible for him, arouses violent anger and anguish in a prophet.

A prophet has unusual sensitivity also to see possibility. Even in the darkest moments. Maybe particularly then. He senses the new that is struggling to be born—in the situations of his life and in his moment of history. He asks, "What new possibility is God offering in this moment of history-making?" He tries to rally men for that. Urges them to leave the rotting past and live contemporarily, i.e., toward the future.

At this point, the prophet turns into history *maker*. He inserts his life into the becoming of his time, and suffers the consequences of trying to make something better become real. So instead of merely enduring history, he makes history. Not that his enterprise immediately succeeds!

DISINHERITED? OR PART OF AN ENTERPRISE TOWARD A DESTINY?

The person who has disinherited himself—or does not feel he has membership in *the people* and the pulsing tradition that has given him his language, lived moments, paradigms, a lore, a culture, a destiny enterprise—is bereft. He is a *patient*, not an *agent*, of civilization, part only of its pathology rather than also of its health.

Rightly we must all be critics, and we have the right to resign from the stinking aspects of the present and the retreating edge of the past. Rightly we scan the weather of coming events to see if a new history-making can be discerned in its tumult. But these must not become evasion of participating.

In medieval days, only a few were permitted to be persons. Only a few had opportunity to take part in creating the culture and meanings by which man lived. Only a few were allowed to make history—the rest suffered it.

A change is taking place. Now we all expect to be persons. Now everyone is to take part in creating public opinion and culture. Now—simultaneously—all over the world we are together making history. What an enterprise!

16

YOUR ONE LIFE ON EARTH

I have tried to state in a fresh way the live options of being human now. Ways which are built into the very nature of *human* life. And are the Judeo-Christian way of civilizing man.

We have not directly talked about such purposes as happiness, pleasure, service to others, achievement, etc.

These vast words have no precise content. They are diffuse and can mean almost anything people want them to mean. They are puffs of wind that mask for us what we really are doing. They enable us to talk beautifully and eloquently *about* life without ever diving into it. We use them more in playing *word games* than in a realistic ethic of life.

HAPPINESS

Happiness—in any realistic, meaningful sense—will be yours as you freely function in the kind of life we have here set forth. Happiness is not so much something you strive directly for as something which comes as a result of. It happens when you are being human, i.e., when you are what you were intended to be. And that we have tried to spell out.

Resolute happiness—a sort of *prevailing* mood of life not altogether a matter of come and go—is what we have been pointing to. By "resolute," we don't mean talking yourself into it, or pumping up your muscles and saying with determination, "Now I am going to get myself a piece of happiness." Resolute means that we can take the bad with the good and still say, "Nevertheless!" For we feel a future in the present, and past memories confirm it.

Tuning in to life in the mode of religious celebration has much to recommend it. "Come hell or high water—I still live in grace and generosity."

PLEASURE

As for pleasure, that is a dead end. If that is what we take for life. Not that we shouldn't have pleasures. But they are incorporated in a meaning of life, in a significance of life. And then they are tremendous. Pleasure is not a significance.

True, there are people—and their number may increase —who rush all over the world looking for a nipple against which they can press their mouths and bodies. They are playboys. Eternal sucklings. Often also they are loud-mouths.

Leisure, comfort, convenience—there's nothing wrong with these either. Until they become mistaken for the goals of life. Until they become the reason why you refuse to share in the suffering of all men, exploit others, and think you are superior clay because you have leisure, comforts, and conveniences. They are accessories. Not the real guts of life. All too easily they can lead you to end up smooth, slick, soft, trying to live on the surfaces of life, separated from world man.

You are a bodied self, not just a body or a "pleasure principle." Along with our whole society, you need to think through, "What is it to actualize such a self?"

Some religious people too long pretended that they were disembodied spirit. Their pretense ruined their religion —since they did not see that love is something embodied. Love is not an emotion but an incarnation. So at least says the Christian faith in its basic document.

Others among us who are pagans think "body" rather than "bodied self." They forget that sex is an act of persons. They treat body hungers as a world apart, not to be governed or suffused by self.

Much present inert education results from the same alienation. Education then becomes something which phony people endure in order to get a well-paying job. Education is felt as something outside the self; certainly outside the transformation of the self. "Forget the self, and learn the mathematics which a computer can use!" But how can we live without a wealth of feeling and cultured meanings? How can we have significance feelings without flesh, glands, eyes, ears, mind, imagination—and a centered self?

We will always have with us misguided people who hate to experience themselves—or others—as self. But . . .

Not pleasure, but a *satisfying* life—one which actualizes our potential to be deeply personal—is goal.

SERVICE TO OTHERS

So we come to service to others as a statement of what life is all about.

This purpose has a long and honorable history. It has brought many good things. It has taught us that we have neighbors and who are our neighbors. That our life should count in something bigger than ourselves. That to limit our life to its own span of time and space is very stupid.

To enable others to become is tremendous.

But "service to others" ducks the question, "to become what? For what purpose is the life of the people you are serving? What is the goal of life?"

You can't just go around altruistically pouring yourself out unless you state to what end, toward what becoming. Life itself has to be valuable. You can't go around "helping people" unless you have some image of what you are helping them *toward*. Just to drag out more years on this earth? Or are you helping them to become *human?* And if so, what do you mean? Even if you say, "I shall minister to them so that they will have life and have it more abundantly," you still have to know what you mean by "life." And you can't give what you yourself don't have.

The world is already too full of people terribly anxious to give themselves to somebody, who have not asked, "But what really worthwhile have I to give? What possibilities of life am I actualizing?" They do not see that they themselves are called to be something greatly. Their "gift" is too puny, questionable. And probably an attempt to escape from life and themselves.

So where are we?

133

CONTINUE BECOMING FRESHLY HUMAN

In this world a great creating and redeeming is going on. We are to participate in it. That is what life is all about.

Participating in this creating and redeeming, we are a *life* world. And live with style.

APPENDIX

A VOCABULARY WITH WHICH TO THINK AND TALK ABOUT HUMAN EXISTENCE

ACTUALIZE

Take on significant shape and function
realize my potential
incarnate truth.
The primal urge within man.

AUTHENTIC

The real article
the good try at being a person
as defined in this book.
Opposite is a life of pretense and duplicity.

CARING

Feeling what is happening
concerned about what can happen
loving. Being *for*.
What man most fundamentally is.

CELEBRATION

Nevertheless!
Come hell or high water
I still live in grace and generosity.
In reverence and appreciation
appropriating the life possible
in my moment of existence.

CO-CREATE

Inventing together
a new enterprise and a new life world

awakening genuine novelty in each other.

Opposite is submission and domination, or indifference.

COMMUNICATION
A two-way interchange
until two or more persons feel they understand something in about the same way.
One of the few fundamental processes.
Finally I must communicate *myself.*

CONSCIENCE
Myself as deeply caring.
Calling me to be authentic to actualize a humane existence.

CREATIVE
Chemicals mix together
and a totally new product emerges.
So might people's minds.
All my life I am creative
unless I am mad at myself.

CREATIVE FIDELITY   See Troth

CULTURE
The meanings
which generations of people have wrested out of life and those they are now manufacturing.

DESTINY
The significance of my life
to something greater than myself.
Being a truth
at some convergence of human journeys.

DEVELOPMENT
Not just getting larger, being more of the same, but a leap

up into a new mode of existence
with a new organizing center.

The past is transformed
and feeds the new future.

EDUCATION

Selected experiences and focused study
by which I actualize my humanness.

Become a bodied *self*
begin to live *in* civilization
some stream of history.

Become a fruitful member
of a democracy
and the new human consciousness.

A project throughout life.

EXPECTANCY

My imagination is intensely active.

Something is not only desirable
but potent enough that it *will* happen.

A mixture of
hope
horizon
celebration.

ENCOUNTER

Meeting someone.

Here he is
and I have to deal with him
as a subject, not as just an object.

EXISTENCE
TO EXIST

What a human being is when
he has some understanding of himself
and the situation he imagines.
Develops it into some particular
form.

Bringing off a life world.

FELLOW MAN   Person I accept as co-creator
                              of a life world.

                  Because
                      I believe in him and in what he be-
                          lieves in
                              feel in common fate with him
                                  we can communicate our-
                                      selves to each other.

FOR   Creative fidelity to the growth of a per-
                      son.

FREEDOM   Being
                      spontaneity
                          spirit
                              a subject.

                  Being
                      in love.

                  Seeing
                      a horizon
                          an opening where I can become.

                  Power
                      to actualize my potential
                          become more than I now am
                              transmute dark moments into
                                  new possibility of good.

GOD   Creating and redeeming
                      constantly going on.

                  Depth. Horizon.
                      More than I will ever know or
                          imagine.

                  Bringing forth sons and a world.

HISTORY

The journey
   of a particular people through time
     and our interpretation of it.

HISTORY-MAKING

Throwing my energies
   into making something better become
     real in some sequence of events.

IMAGINATION

Imaging
   new possibility
     and *new time.*

A most potent agent of all persons' development.

IN

Not
   contained in.

But
   participating in.

With and in.

INCARNATE

Be a truth
   with spine and muscle.
     Don't just talk about it.

I-IT

Two "its"
   joined in an impersonal way
     by natural urges
       or monologue.

I-THOU

Subject-subject
   encountering the other
     as a living free system
       within a larger system in which
         we both participate.

INVOKE

"Come out of the depths of mystery
   and *be.*

Be *with me.*"

LIFE WORLD

The meaningful world of persons,
   things, events
    which the possibilities I see
      organize out of the whole world.
The special habitat of life
    as far as I am concerned.
      I am in it too.
Self-in-world.

LOVE

Deeply caring plus
   understanding plus
     creative fidelity plus
       communication plus
        I-Thou.

MANIFEST

Take off the masks
   the disguises
     the pretense
       the duplicity
And appear.
Come out of the fog
   and take shape.
Be present
   stand up and be counted.
The days of playing games
   e.g. peek-a-boo
     are over.

MEANING

My contribution
   to something greater than I am.
My sense
   of an opening into a future that is
     desirable.

My report
    that something is enlivening or dead-
       ening me and what I care for.

I can live as a human being
    only in a meaningful world.

OBJECT

Nonpersonal material
    to be fashioned
       in terms of my purposes.

The It of I-It
    A thingified person.

PARADIGM
EXPERIENCE

An experiencing
    where the meaning of life breaks
       through to me and my people.

An organizer of my life.

The culture and tradition in which I
    live is made up of paradigms.

PARTICIPATE

"The fish is in the ocean
    and the ocean is in the fish."

I am *present*
    not a spectator or on-looker.

Inserting myself
    into some sequence of history-making.

POSSIBILITY

Potential
    seen
       recognized for what it is
          given the green light.

POTENTIAL

Originative ocean
    genes not yet actualized
       something's push to develop.

What a becoming world
  as contrasted to a static world
    is filled with. And *is*.

PUBLIC OPINION

An amorphous, anonymous
  cloud of attitude and interpretation
    a world of culture.

We all live in it
  and might help shape it.

RISK

"For the sake of"

Some possibility together with my troth
  ought to be actualized.

Someone has to move it.

I cannot know ahead of time all the consequences but I dive
    swimming as more light breaks
      through to me.

SIGNIFICANT
SYMBOL

An important event or meaning
  which people talk about enough
    and risk enough life on
      that it finally means about the
      same to everyone
        dependably calling forth a
        similar response.

Without significant symbol
  there is no
    society, no
      me.

SPONTANEITY

Exuberant freedom
  able to do the relevant
    in the situation.

Not
    on-the-moment id impulses
      of anger or lust.

STYLE

Uncluttered
    achievement of some purpose
characteristic and distinctive
    of me
Has nothing to do with
    "the fashion of the week."

SUBJECT

An *originating* center of aliveness
    not the object of *my* verb.
The Thou and the I in I-Thou
    not a conditioned response.

TRADITION

A distinctive style of existence
    setting out through time
      toward a destiny.

TROTH

A choice which has length to it
    and no reservations.
Many choices and experiences come out
    of it.
Troth is creative fidelity to each other's
    growth and to joint enterprise.

TRUTH

The potential
    that creates and redeems the world.
The potential
    of the Kingdom of God.
Hidden
    in each situation I find myself in.
I know TRUTH
    only to the degree I participate in it.

143

Truth

My participation
 in the heres and nows
  in TRUTH.
Only truth
 can know TRUTH.

UNDERSTANDING

Comprehending the other person as
 truth.

Receiving a person *as he is*
 right here and now
and not as I want him to be
 or previously thought him to be.

Entering into and standing inside his
 existence
 not being overcome by it
  but able to symbolize its complexi-
   ties and some possibility in it.